PRAISING YOU
Changes Me

A Business Traveler's Divine Moments on the Road

Sheryl R. Sellaway

WESTBOW
PRESS®
A DIVISION OF THOMAS NELSON
& ZONDERVAN

THE HOLY BIBLE, NEW INTERNATIONAL VERSION®, NIV® Copyright © 1973, 1978, 1984, 2011 by Biblica, Inc.® Used by permission. All rights reserved worldwide.

WestBow Press books may be ordered through booksellers or by contacting:

WestBow Press
A Division of Thomas Nelson & Zondervan
1663 Liberty Drive
Bloomington, IN 47403
www.westbowpress.com
1 (866) 928-1240

ISBN: 978-1-5127-7661-4 (sc)
ISBN: 978-1-5127-7662-1 (hc)
ISBN: 978-1-5127-7660-7 (e)

Library of Congress Control Number: 2017902812

Print information available on the last page.

WestBow Press rev. date: 03/22/2017

Trust in the Lord with all your heart and lean not on your own understanding; in all your ways submit to him and he will make your path straight.

—Proverbs 3:5–6

You are worthy, our Lord and our God, to receive glory and honor and power, for you created all things, and by your will they were created and have their being.

—Revelation 4:11

This book is dedicated to the Lord Almighty.
You deserve all the honor, all the glory, all the praise.

Contents

Preface

I live in Atlanta. And yet in overnight stays for one, two, or three days at a time, I've spent the night in many cities in the South and across the country. In a manner of speaking, I've lived in many places and stayed in all kinds of hotels during my business travel over the years—some quaint; others nice, elaborate, or ordinary; and a few I'll probably never visit again.

During my times of travel, I've visited cities too numerous to count. Most trips I take by plane. However, I have been known to hop in the car on occasion for a trip that is only a couple of hours away. Whether near or far, my past travel was normal. From the world's standpoint, I would leave home to travel to a city, stay overnight in a hotel, attend or host a meeting, and return home. I experienced the usual flight delays, cancellations, lost bags, hotel mix-ups, an upgrade here and there, friendly and grumpy travelers, hospitable people at the many airports, customer service issues, crowded rental car buses, junk food, poor restaurant service, the best of the best places to dine, a great view from a hotel room, a view of the parking lot of a hotel room, and jet lag. The list goes on.

However, from a spiritual point of view, my travel was anything but normal. I had many memorable encounters with strangers and situations that were divine opportunities to grow my faith. On countless occasions, the Lord placed on my path—sometimes very quickly—situations and circumstances that called for me to trust Him completely, pray without ceasing, experience miracles, minister to others and be ministered to, learn an important lesson, take a close look at my actions and the actions of others, and stand up for the Word of God. The thread woven through most of these situations was an acknowledgment of the Lord's presence.

I have a pesky habit of taking my tattered and worn *Dr. Charles F. Stanley Life Principles Daily Bible* with me when I travel. In spite of my many faults and failures, this action—taking the Lord on the road with me, so to speak—is one of the best, most fruitful decisions I have ever made. Actually, I'd like to *blame* the Bible and its mere presence for some of the divine experiences I had while on the road. You see, on some of my flights, the Bible's presence led to conversations I would never have had. It caused me to reflect on my travels and pray about my issues and challenges—personal and professional. Without the Bible, I am not sure I would have been of sound mind and body during some of my most difficult moments. Most importantly, the countless opportunities to pray, study, and praise the Lord changed me immensely. The Bible can change you too!

I crafted these God-ordained stories to share with you the tremendous lessons I learned from strangers I encountered during my travels. I hope these intriguing, heartfelt stories along with my prayers and praises will cause you to think about your own encounters of the divine kind. The questions that accompany each story will give you opportunities to reflect on how you can relate to the situation, consider your own potential actions, and ponder how you would handle a similar encounter in the future. There's also an opportunity for you to craft a prayer after each story—to give you divine inspiration—along with the Lord's intervention. What could be better than that? For me, it starts with praising the Lord. Just praise ... and listen. "Whether you turn to the right or to the left, your ears will hear a voice behind you saying, This is the way; walk in it" (Isaiah 30:21).

CHAPTER 1

Why Praising You Changes Me

Come, let us sing for joy to the Lord; let us shout aloud to the Rock of our Salvation. Let us come before him with thanksgiving and extol him with music and song. For the Lord is the great God, the great King above all gods. In his hand are the depths of the earth, and the mountain peaks belong to him. The sea is his, for he made it, and his hands formed the dry land. Come, let us bow down in worship, let us kneel before the Lord our Maker; for he is our God and we are the people of his pasture, and flock under his care.

—Psalm 95:1–7 (NIV)

ISN'T IT AMAZING that it is hard to complain and to praise God at the same time? That's right—something incredibly supernatural happens when we praise the Lord, whether we pray, sing a song, or tell others about Jesus. It is really hard to be mad, angry, upset, or linger in unforgiveness and at the same time recall all that God has done for you. Think about all the times God has answered your prayers—small, medium, or large. Think about all the times He has shown you time and time again that He is near you and all the times He has healed you, sealed you in His divine protection, and prevented something bad from happening to you. In fact, remember that time He brought to mind something critically important on a notable date on your calendar? Remember that action item or meeting you almost forgot? How do you think that happened?

I don't know about you, but for me something joyous happens when I start a prayer with praise. There is something meaningful about when the sunshine hits my face and I can praise the Creator. Something happens when you have a list of needs and yet start with praise. Much like you start a conversation with a friend—saying hello before you start in on your problems—God wants us to approach Him like a dear friend with our thanksgiving first ... and with praise.

What I've found over time is that praising the Lord changes me. I'm more grateful and more thankful, and I want to just enjoy the Lord's presence. I want to hear from the Lord rather than be heard. I want to understand rather than be understood. I want to be still, at peace, and just soak up His presence. How do you think that happened? When I see God's hand in these little things, when I start a prayer by saying, "Thank You, Lord," something joyous happens.

How often do you thank the Lord for His many provisions? For me, not often enough. Do you give credit to almighty God for all He has done, or do you give yourself credit for being so smart? For me, not enough.

How often do you praise the Lord for the innumerable ways in which He has shown you unconditional love? For the sunshine, for the rain, for fresh air, for waking you up? How often do you give credit to the Creator—and not to the creation—for that beautiful view of the mountain that took your breath away? What about for the rain that grew those vegetables on your dinner table? Or that storm where you ran and hid, afraid of the unknown, when God kept you and your family safe? Again, for me, not enough. These questions are all reminders of God's endless love for us. In fact, God's endless flow of love blows me away, for He loves us even when we reject Him and even when we let Him down and pretend we don't know Him. He loves us even when we shun Him, and he loves us even when we not only disobey Him but when we do the exact opposite of what He says for our own selfish, limited purposes. Who else gives you unfailing love in this awesome way? He corrects us but doesn't condemn us. He disciplines us but doesn't desert us. He just wants us to be His. And the good news is that He will move heaven and earth to accomplish His will for our lives—which is best. "He who began a good work in you will carry it on to completion until the day of Christ Jesus" (Philippians 1:6).

For all of these shining attributes and so much more, He deserves honor, praise, and glory.

Are you running ahead of God, asking Him to bless your plans rather than seeking Him for the plans He has for you? Just remember that if it's not in God's will, it won't be beneficial to you in the future—and sometimes it all turns to ashes. "Many are the plans in a person's heart, but it is the Lord's purpose that prevails" (Proverbs 19:21).

As you praise the Lord, recall the many times God answered your prayers—and in ways that were so unique that you could only praise Him. Or remember the time He didn't answer right away. You felt dry, parched, and deeply concerned about the future. Without that answered prayer, what would you do? And yet you waited ... and waited ... and waited. Then all of a sudden, it came, and at the absolutely right time. All you could do was praise God, and it grew your faith yet again. Always remember that delay is God's providential hand of protection. "Since ancient times no one has heard, no ear has perceived, no eye has seen any God besides you, who acts on behalf of those who wait for him" (Isaiah 64:4).

Praise, Worship, Trust, and Wait

How often in a day's time do you praise the Lord—no matter where you are? How often do you give credit where credit is due? For me, not often enough. Some people might not know what I am talking about because it's not just singing, clapping, and celebrating, although it can be those things. However, it's more than that—much more. It is fellowship with the Lord. It is studying God's Word, being obedient, and taking the time to listen to God. It is striving to be truthful, treating others the way we want to be treated, caring about others, and doing what's right, even when it is hard. These are the attributes God wants of us as His children. It is giving all glory, honor, and praise to the Lord Almighty. Believe it or not, God wants us to experience life through the lens of His Word. Always remember that there are no accidents in the kingdom of God. "Yours, Lord, is the greatness and the power and the glory and the majesty and the splendor, for everything in heaven and earth is yours. Yours, Lord, is the kingdom; you are exalted as head over all" (1 Chronicles 29:11).

When you open your eyes in the morning, who do you thank? Do you thank anybody, or do you rush about forgetting the breath, the strength, and the mobility that God so generously gave you so that you could rise for another day? What we should do is open our eyes and immediately praise the Lord for another day. We should worship the Lord for another day of life. We should worship the Lord by spending time in prayer to acknowledge Him first and foremost.

What's amazing is that we trust the Lord even without realizing it. We just do. We trust Him for the big things—for the sun rising and setting and for the moon staying affixed in the sky. And as much as we complain about it, we trust the rain to fall and give us the water we need to live. We trust that flowers will bloom, butterflies will flutter, and birds will sing. And yet we struggle with trusting God for healing, for better lives, for positive changes in our relationships, and for answers to our laundry list of prayers. Do we know this Lord we serve? Can we trust God to hear us and to answer our prayers? I say a resounding yes! That's because He is the sovereign God of the universe. He knows what's best for us. "Do not be anxious about anything, but in every situation, by prayer and petition, with thanksgiving, present your requests to God. And the peace of God which transcends all understanding, will guard your hearts and your minds in Christ Jesus" (Philippians 4:6–7).

A Prayer of Praising, Worshipping, Trusting, and Waiting upon the Lord

As you wait upon the Lord, here is a prayer of encouragement for your journey.

> Help us, Lord, to get to the place where we want for ourselves what You want for us. Help us, Lord, to sincerely want Your will to be done, not ours. Help us to check in with You before we cast our plans into stone. For Lord, You have shown us time and time again that Your ways are so much higher than our ways. Your will for our lives is absolutely the best there is.
>
> Over time I have found out that if I praise, worship, and trust—and wait—I get Your best, Lord. I get to see You

work in many ways that, as it turns out, can't be imagined in my wildest dreams. It is unfathomable.

When we praise You, Lord, we should know by now—especially if we know You as Lord and Savior—that we are in fellowship with You. Thank You, Lord, for the lovely gift and the magnificence of praise and worship. It changes me, for it is in Your presence that I become what You want me to be. It is not a quick fix or a simple step. Rather it is a complex endeavor. It cleanses. It heals. And it is supernatural. Thank You, Lord, for the countless opportunities to praise, worship, trust, and wait upon you. Amen.

Praise the Lord through Your Circumstances

I know it sounds odd to some, but as we grow in our faith, we learn to praise the Lord through our changing circumstances—through the storms of life, the valleys, and the insurmountable difficulties. It is incredibly hard to praise the Lord when you're grieving, when your relationship's in trouble, or when your kids are in trouble. And yet you should not focus on the issue. Instead, focus on praising the Lord. That's because as you praise Him, He will guide and direct your path through that issue, through that gut-wrenching challenge, or through that situation that is so difficult. He is our Comforter. And whatever the issue is, He is the solution. He knew about it long before you were born. He knows your beginning, your middle, and your end.

Is the Lord quiet in your life right now? If you're waiting to hear from Him, consider this: He might be working on you first before He speaks to your heart and before He answers that prayer. Perhaps He's pruning you, cleaning you up, or testing you before that next big assignment. God wants you to be ready. And He wants you to trust Him and His steadfast, unfailing, unshakable love for you that transcends your sins, faults, and past mistakes.

I am the true vine, and my Father is the gardener. He cuts off every branch in me that bears no fruit, while every branch that does not bear fruit he prunes so that it will be even more fruitful. You are already clean because of the word I have spoken to you. Remain in me, and I also remain in you. No branch can bear fruit by itself; it must remain in the vine. Neither can you bear fruit unless you remain in me. I am the vine; you are the branches. If you remain in me and I in you, you will bear much fruit; apart from me you can do nothing. (John 15:1–5)

Proverbs 3:5–6 says, "Trust in the Lord with all your heart." That means all, not some. It says trust in the Lord, not in your job, your family, or your friends. Through your trust in the Lord, He might direct you to your family or a friend. However, He wants you to seek Him first. At times I picked up the phone to call a friend after an issue. I recall on a couple of occasions, the phone jammed, and I couldn't make a call. That was the Lord saying, "Sheryl, talk to Me first!" The verse goes on to say, "And lean not on your own understanding." In other words, don't look to yourself to best understand a situation. Don't rest on your emotions or your will because you're limited. God is unlimited. The verse continues, "In all your ways acknowledge Him." It says all, not some. There is a promise there. "And He will make your path straight." It says that *He* will make your path straight, not your spouse, your employer, or your friend. He's not just concerned about one issue. God is bigger than that. He is interested in your path, your direction, your journey, not just singular issues. The key is to make Jesus your all—your heart, your acknowledgment, and your obedience. He'll take care of the rest!

How Does the Lord Reach You?

Oftentimes the Lord reached me on the road because that is where He could speak to me—while I was traveling. And as a simple person, He could reach me through strangers I interacted with on the road. In some cases, He had my undivided attention. I was sitting on a plane with nowhere else to go! Later, when I really opened my eyes, I discovered He was reaching me everywhere. God was teaching me, growing me up, and removing the impurities from my life so that I could serve Him obediently. Did you know that obedience can be painful?

Where is God reaching you? At work, at home with your family, through a club or organization, at your church? Here's hoping He's reaching you in all of these places and more. God will seek to reach you where He has the best chance of impacting you and others. It is where He will teach you, mold you, and potentially cause you to deal with old wounds that need healing or help others with their wounds. He will cause you to help others see the light or shine a light on their darkness perhaps. At times He will do radical work, using you to share the gospel in places where it is not welcome, perhaps even hostile. Are you willing to pay a high price for standing up for the Lord? It could cost you. Do you have what it takes? Have you ever lost a job or friends? Have you been uninvited places? Has your name been taken off of lists, not considered for certain jobs, unwelcome in the clique, or removed from the contact list all because of your faith? If you answered yes, take heart! God is trusting you to shine a light in difficult places. Don't worry about the outcome. He's got that covered. He's got the light. You might not know the whole story for some time. Just know that God is reaching you and teaching you. And He is using you to reach others for the kingdom of God. There's no more important work than that. That's why it is so painful. God will take care of the pain. After all, He is the divine healer, the CEO of the universe, the Great Physician who is righteous, holy, omnipotent, merciful, faithful, and sovereign. If He can't heal you, nobody can! "Join with me in suffering, like a good soldier of Christ Jesus" (2 Timothy 2:3).

It's almost like spreading germs. God will allow you to meet people and impact them or be impacted by them. Then you're changed, and you allow that experience to impact someone else. Spreading the love of God is not just for preachers. It goes on and on. That's why it's so important to seek Him first. He'll cleanse you in all areas of your life so that you can experience the righteousness that only He can make possible in your life. God wants others to look in the mirror of your life and see a reflection of Him. "If the root is holy, so are the branches" (Romans 11:16).

Are you going through something very difficult, a matter that's life-altering, excruciatingly painful, something that has rocked you to the core? Has your faith been shaken like never before? Just know that God is fully aware of the depth and breadth of your suffering. Believe it or not, He allowed those circumstances. After all, He is the sovereign God of the universe. He could have stepped in. Perhaps He is allowing you to face certain consequences. He could be shaping and molding you for big plans in the future. He may want you to have the muscle, the stamina, and the will to handle that divine assignment. Whatever the purpose, He allowed that difficulty—not to destroy you or tear you down but to build you up for the future. When you look out the window of your life, refuse to see anything but God's hand, which is working all things together for your good (for those who love Him). Trust that the God, who made you, will keep you. Refuse to doubt that God is in control. Believe that He will watch over you, direct you, and accomplish His purpose in you. He is your anchor. Don't give up on the Lord as He would never give up on you. Praise Him. He'll change you. Be warned though. It's hard work to trust in the Lord beyond your circumstances. Giving up is much easier! "Though the fig tree does not bud and there are no grapes on the vines, though the olive crop fails and the fields produce no food, though there are no sheep in the pen and no cattle in the stalls, yet I will rejoice in the Lord, I will be joyful in my Savior. The Sovereign Lord is my strength; he makes my feet like the feet of a deer, he enables me to tread on the heights" (Habakkuk 3:17–19).

Missed Opportunities

While I am sharing with you a few interesting moments on the road, most of them with great insight, what you won't find here are the countless missed opportunities. That's because I missed them. Unfortunately, the missed opportunities are too numerous to count. For every person I prayed with or prayed for, there were many others I dismissed because I was too busy, too self-absorbed, or too focused on that next journey. So for the record, I have plenty of work to do—to reach people who need help, people who need Jesus. *Lord, help me to be more attentive to the needs of Your people in a busy, hectic world.* Please enjoy these stories, pray about how God would have you respond in similar situations, and look for divine moments in your own life! "Therefore, my dear brothers, stand firm. Let nothing move you. Always give yourselves fully to the work of the Lord, because you know that your labor in the Lord is not in vain" (1 Corinthians 15:58).

CHAPTER 2

The Crown

Whoever has ears, let him hear.
—Matthew 11:15

I HAD WORK TO do. I was in the Delta Air Lines Crown Room (now known as the Sky Club), a rather nice one with spacious seating areas, and in a corner there were individualized booths where you could power up your computer, enjoy a snack, and take some alone time. I found an empty booth, sat down, opened my laptop, pulled out a few folders, and began to work. I could hear people talking. In fact, I heard a couple of guys exchanging insights about the wireless industry, so my ears opened wide. However, I decided it was best to stay out of that conversation.

In the distance I heard various other noises and chattering. Then I could hear what I thought was a woman crying. I must admit that at first I did keep working, thinking the crying would stop. However, the sobs grew louder and louder. Surely, someone would go over to the booth and ask this lady if she was okay. It didn't happen. The sobs continued and grew louder and more desperate. "I am not going over there," I said to myself. Why is everybody here ignoring her? Am I the only one who can hear her crying? The crying was now loud and hard to ignore. I could feel a nudge in my spirit, tugging at my heart to go over to where the woman was sitting. I said to myself on the inside, "Lord, do I have to go over there?" I knew the answer. I hesitated for a moment. I went over to the woman and sat next to her.

"Excuse me. I don't know you, but I heard you crying. Do you mind if I just pray with you for a moment?" I said. I caught her in the middle of a sob.

She swallowed and said, "Yes." I took that to mean she wanted me to pray with her. I could smell alcohol on her breath, and yet her disposition didn't signal to me that she was having a "I had too much to drink and life's bad" kind of cry. Something was definitely wrong. I felt in my spirit I should pray with her, console her, and not play therapist. I decided it was best not to ask any questions. So I reached out for her hand, and she grabbed it, squeezed it tight, and didn't let go. Her hands were warm and sweaty. She continued to weep, but more calmly. I figured most people know the Lord's Prayer and Psalm 23. I chose to say a brief prayer and close with the Lord's Prayer. We said the words slowly together,

> Our Father, which art in heaven, hallowed be Thy name.
> Thy kingdom come, Thy will be done in earth as it is in
> heaven.
> Give us this day our daily bread.
> And forgive us our debts, as we forgive our debtors.
> And lead us not into temptation, but deliver us from evil:
> For Thine is the kingdom, and the power, and the glory,
> forever. Amen. (Based on Matthew 6:9–13 KJV)

When we finished, she proclaimed that I was an angel in her time of need and thanked me profusely.

Maybe, just maybe I was the only one who heard her cry or chose to hear it that day. In that moment I knew God had scheduled an appointment for me with a very downhearted woman in the Delta Crown Room.

My Prayer and Praise: *Lord, thank You for drawing me near to You so I could answer Your cry and hers too. I praise You, Lord, for giving me ears to hear and a heart in this case to obey.*

Questions to Ponder: When was the last time you saw someone in trouble but refused to help? For the record, we all have these moments. Perhaps you felt you didn't have time, you might be in danger, or you just didn't want to potentially complicate your life. What will you do next time you see someone in need?

Your Prayer: Craft a prayer for your next potential opportunity to help someone else. Ask the Lord to guide, direct, and order your steps so that you will seek to reach, help, and serve others.

CHAPTER 3

Watch Out

You are the God who performs miracles; you display your
power among the peoples.

—Psalm 77:14.

EVEN WITH A couple of hours' preparation, the heavy traffic in Atlanta
can cause even the most prepared, patient traveler to sigh, moan,
and complain. When I arrived at the Hartsfield-Jackson International
Airport, I knew I could get to my terminal and gate on time. But I didn't
have any time to spare. I couldn't afford to stop on the way to my gate
or address any last-minute issues. I didn't want to risk missing my flight.

I went through security, taking off the usual items—shoes, jacket,
bracelet, and watch. I placed my bracelet and watch in one of those gray
security bowls. I am not sure if security encouraged it or if it was my bright
idea. Nonetheless, I placed all of my items on the conveyer belt, walked
through the security device, got the nod from TSA, and collected my
items on the other end. After I pulled myself together, I proceeded down
the escalator and on to the train. I rode two stops on the train and then
noticed my arm was bare. Yikes! *Where is my beloved watch? My favorite
watch with the pink face?* I left it behind at security. It's not like the airport
would page me. They didn't know who owned the watch! Travelers leave
items behind all the time. The airport's lost and found probably looks like
your local resale shop.

I had a choice to make—run back and try to find my watch or miss
my flight. I didn't feel I had enough time to run after the watch and catch

my flight. Before I could think twice, I said to myself quickly, "I'm going back to find my watch!"

So I leaped into action, jumping off the train. I ran back to security. I found my way back and told the security person on duty that I left an item behind, and she let me through, which pleasantly surprised me. I walked over to the security line I had just left a few minutes before. I asked one of the TSA officers about my watch. A gentleman suggested I go to the security desk—a rather large desk located in the center of the security area. I approached a lady and told her I left a watch behind while going through security. She asked me to describe it. I did. She reached under the desk and produced my beloved watch and bracelet. I completely forgot about the bracelet. The lady said, "A nice man who was behind you brought the items over to us. You're very lucky." What she was trying to say is this action doesn't always take place. I thanked her, and then I realized I had a flight to catch. This time around I really had to make a run for it. I zipped down the escalator, hopped on the train, and literally ran all the way to the gate. I arrived at the gate just in the nick of time. And I got an upgrade! Can you believe that?

My prayer along the way to the gate was simple. *Lord, help me find my watch and help me make my flight.* When God answers prayer, He always exceeds our expectations!

My Prayer and Praise: *Lord, I praise You for how You answer all kinds of prayers—even a prayer about a watch and a flight. You have a way, Lord, of answering prayer that is exceedingly and abundantly more than we can imagine.*

Questions to Ponder: Do you have an item of value that you lost? When you found it, did you give credit to God, yourself, or the person who found it? Consider the parable of the lost coin. "Or suppose a woman has ten silver coins and loses one. Does she not light a lamp, sweep the house and search carefully until she finds it? And when she finds it, she calls her friends and neighbors together and says, 'Rejoice with me, I have found my lost coin.' In the same way, I tell you there is rejoicing in the presence of the angels of God over one sinner who repents" (Luke 15:8–10).

Your Prayer: Craft a prayer thanking the Lord for an answer to a prayer about something you lost but found. Just as the woman was joyous about finding the one lost coin, the angels in heaven rejoice every time one sinner repents!

CHAPTER 4

Precious Feet

For you created my inmost being; you knit me together
in my mother's womb.

—Psalm 139:13

ON A FLIGHT from Tampa to Atlanta, I sat next to a cheery, happy young woman. I was digging in my purse and pulled out a card with a small pair of gold feet—a pin attached to a card. It was placed in the pocket of my purse to remind me about life. However, I forgot it was there, and so when I pulled it out, I paused to review it once again. The card, which was called Precious Feet, is designed to show you the exact size and shape of a ten-week old unborn baby's feet. The card also includes facts about the unborn. When I pulled it out, the woman said, "I have one of those too!" From there, we struck up a great conversation about the sanctity of life.

What was amazing about our conversation was the fact that that very week I had been thinking about the aftermath of a decision I made to discontinue my affiliation with an organization because of their disposition about this very issue, life. This was no chance meeting—sitting next to a woman who obviously values life. In fact, it felt like confirmation that I made the right decision.

My Prayer and Praise: *Thank You, Lord, for the reminder that life is precious. Help me, Lord, not to ever forget about the sanctity of human life. Amen.*

Question to Ponder: Do you value life? In what way?

Your Prayer: Write a short prayer that honors the gift of life. Here are a few scripture passages from the Bible about life.

- "Before I formed you in the womb I knew you" (Jeremiah 1:5).
- "For you created my inmost being; you knit me together in my mother's womb. I praise you because I am fearfully and wonderfully made" (Psalm 139:13–14).
- "In his hand is the life of every creature and the breath of all mankind" (Job 12:10).
- "Don't you know that you yourselves are God's temple and that God's Spirit dwells in your midst? If anyone destroys God's temple, God will destroy that person; for God's temple is sacred, and you together are that temple" (1 Corinthians 3:16–17).

CHAPTER 5

Expect Miracles

Truly I tell you, if you have faith as small as a mustard seed, you can say to this mountain, "Move from here to there" and it will move. Nothing will be impossible for you.

—Matthew 17:20

I've HAD SEVERAL flat tire incidents over the years. In this case, I was traveling down a busy, crowded highway. It was just a normal day of rush-hour traffic on Georgia 400. I was going about fifty-five or so miles per hour when my car started to slow down without my help. It took me a few minutes to realize I had a flat tire. I was amongst a highway full of cars. I was in the far left lane, and then something happened.

I looked in my rearview mirror and noticed that I had a clear path to move from the far left lane all the way over to the emergency lane. Don't ask me how it happened as it happened rather quickly. I just know that God saw fit for me to get from one side of the highway to the other in record time. He literally separated me from all the traffic on the highway to get me safely off of the highway. I called for help from man *after* I received divine intervention from God.

On another occasion, I was traveling to Savannah over a Memorial Day weekend. It was a Saturday in the late morning. I made a smoothie and hit the road. While traveling down I-75 between Dublin and Savannah, I heard a noise. I soon discovered it was a flat tire. I pulled over into the emergency lane. I got out, looked at the condition of the tire, and decided that I shouldn't try to drive the car at all in order to keep from damaging the rim. I sat in the car for a few minutes and called emergency road service. It was a holiday weekend, and so they had to dispatch for local service. It would take at least thirty to forty-five minutes. I decided at that moment I couldn't wait that long. You see, I had that giant smoothie, and so now I was getting a clear call from nature. Talk about bad timing. While I didn't want to leave my car on the side of road, I decided I had no choice. I was probably about a quarter of a mile from the next exit, so I decided to sprint to the convenience store just off of the exit. I grabbed my purse and made a jog for it. Cars passed. No one stopped to ask if I needed help. Frankly, in this day and age, I wasn't surprised or upset about it. Just before I reached the store, a man driving a towing service truck did stop me to ask if I left my car on the highway. However, at that time, I wasn't sure if he was inquiring about my car as a result of the call I had placed to roadside assistance. I wasn't about to get into a truck with a stranger in the middle of nowhere.

I walked into the convenience store, used the restroom, and felt so much better. As I made my way back to my car, a Georgia State Patrol officer pulled up next to me and asked if I left my car on the highway. "Yes, that's my car," I said.

"You should never leave your car on the highway like that," he said.

I was embarrassed to say this, but I did. "I didn't have a choice. I had to go to the restroom," I said.

"I'll give you a ride back to your car," he said. As I slid into the backseat of the patrol car, it was my hope that this was my first and last time riding in a police car. The officer seemed very kind. In fact, he gave me a ride back to my car, waited for the tow truck, and remained with me until my spare tire was on the car and I was ready to hit the road. By the way, the towing service I encountered on the walk to the convenience store was indeed the correct towing service. To me, the towing service driver was a stranger. The officer was not. I felt I could trust him. This officer was chivalrous, friendly, and caring. I was so thankful that even on a holiday weekend, he took interest in a citizen stranded on the highway with a flat tire. His timing was perfect.

My Prayer and Praise: *Lord, thank You for the reminder that You are the God of the universe. You have the power to do anything You want to do in record time. Your timing is always perfect. Thank You for taking such good care of me.*

Question to Ponder: Can you recall a time when something miraculous happened to you? It couldn't be explained or justified. It was God.

Your Prayer: Write a prayer thanking the Lord for that miracle and for those yet to come!

CHAPTER 6

The Giant in the Middle

The Lord does not look at the things people looks at.
People look at the outward appearance, but the Lord looks
at the heart.

—1 Samuel 16:7

DO YOU BELIEVE God has a sense of humor? I do. He often has a funny way of teaching you, showing you, and expanding your view, including certain situations you might find uncomfortable. These situations will cause you to look at yourself in the mirror—perhaps accept others you might find challenging to deal with. I was on a flight to Orange County, California, ultimately planning to drive from Orange County to Palm Springs. It's not a bad drive. Actually, it's a chance to unwind and transition from work mode to vacation mode. I just had to survive the four-hour flight from Atlanta to Orange County.

I got on the plane. The hope is to sit next to someone who's not too obtrusive, doesn't talk too much or wants to place their head on my shoulder. Well, I sat down in my usual aisle seat. People are walking down the aisle. And then I see this guy who looks like the Jolly Green Giant personified. He is walking down the aisle. I am saying to myself, *Wow. Oh no. No. God, no. How is that man going to sit in this seat?*

Sure enough, he said. "I am sitting there." I stepped out into the aisle, and as it turned out, he had the middle (center) seat. The man folded himself into the seat and sat down. The man had to sit literally with his arms folded for the entire flight. I mean, his arms were almost in midair like a genie. He must have been very uncomfortable—much more uncomfortable than I was that day. I survived. And he turned out to be a very nice gentleman.

On the return flight, I sat down. As I was getting comfortable, I saw the Jolly Green Giant again. He was coming my way. *Oh no, not again.* He saw me and said, "Hey, we were on the same flight last time." He smiled and walked on by. It wouldn't have been so bad again, especially since he was much more uncomfortable than I was. And he was a nice person.

My Prayer and Praise: *Lord, help me to be more flexible. Through Your humor, You showed me that the world You created is made up of all kinds of people who just want a seat. I praise You for all the lessons I learn from You. And Lord help me to resist judging people because of their appearance.*

Questions to Ponder: Have you ever judged someone or perhaps misjudged someone because of their outer appearance? What was the lesson for you?

Your Prayer: Craft a prayer that reminds you to see everyone as God's child.

CHAPTER 7

Favorite Things

Moreover, when God gives someone wealth and possessions, and the ability to enjoy them, to accept their lot and be happy in their toil—this is a gift of God.

—Ecclesiastes 5:19

GOD CARES ABOUT all the details of our lives. He knows it all. That's why He sends rain to care for flowers, places friends in our lives at just the right time, and gives us all kinds of pleasures to enjoy. That's to enjoy, not to idolize. He is even aware of our favorite things—like my favorite bracelet.

One day I looked for the bracelet and simply couldn't find it. I did ask around at the places I had visited recently. Initially, I came to the conclusion that it was lost. However, I decided I needed to stop thinking about it and just let it rest. I prayed about it and felt that the bracelet would turn up at some point. When I let the bracelet go in my mind and focused on more important matters, it showed up in my suitcase.

My Prayer and Praise: *Lord, thank You for calling on me to let go and let God. You manage all of the details of my life—even a lost bracelet. Thank You for helping me to focus on more important matters and later find what was lost. More important than the bracelet was the reminder to let go and let God.*

Question to Ponder: Have you ever lost something that was a favorite thing and then later found it only after you stopped thinking about it and focused on more important matters?

Your Prayer: Thank the Lord for that favorite thing. He gave it to you!

CHAPTER 8

More Than a Cough

Trust in him at all times, you people; pour out your hearts
to him, for God is our refuge.

—Psalm 62:8

I TRAVELED BY CAR to the home of an educator for a reception to
network with college students, encourage them, and hear a few success
stories. The event was a gathering of students, professors, administrators,
and supporters.

The home was spacious with a large living area made up of sofas,
chairs, and coffee tables. The guests gathered in this area—some sitting,
others standing around. Most of the students gathered in the kitchen with
the food, but some guests were spilling out into the informal dining area.
In essence, people gathered throughout the home.

An elderly couple sat on the sofa in the living area. The wife began
to cough lightly. She drank water and continued to cough. After a few
minutes, I grew concerned. Her coughing continued with more intensity.
Her husband seemed helpless. He didn't seem to know what to do. He
wasn't alone though. The people around him just sat there as she struggled
to maintain her composure. Meanwhile, in the kitchen the students
continued chatting and laughing. It wasn't intentional. They just didn't
know what was going on in the living area.

The woman obviously had something lodged in her throat. Should we
continue to let her cough and hope she's better soon? Though she was a
stranger, I was deeply concerned about her life, so I asked if I could try the

Heimlich maneuver to help dislodge whatever was trapped in her throat. I did. She seemed better, but I still insisted we call 911. The woman said she was okay, and her husband seemed to agree. But I just wasn't comfortable with that. I started praying. During a crisis we don't have a lot of time to ponder what's next. We just need prayer with action. I walked into the kitchen and chatted with the host, insisting that we call 911. She did.

The paramedics came quickly. The woman reluctantly left with them. She began to cough again as she was departing. I called to check on her the next day and learned that she was admitted to the hospital. Apparently, she had emergency surgery because she had something lodged in her esophagus. Had the woman not gone to the hospital as we insisted, she mostly likely would not have survived. If left up to you and others, your life—and mine—could be over in seconds. We have to pray and trust God in our time of great need.

My Prayer and Praise: *Thank You, Lord, for the power of prayer, the ability to keep calm in the midst of a crisis, and for helping me to go with what was in my spirit—pray and call 911. The signal came from You, Lord. I thank You, Lord, for saving that woman's life. It was not yet this elderly woman's time to leave this earth.*

Questions to Ponder: Have you ever been thrust into a situation where someone's life was in danger?

Your Prayer: Write a prayer asking the Lord to guide you not *if* but *when* you have to act with only a few seconds to make a decision. Ask for courage, calmness, and divine direction.

CHAPTER 9

Plastic Angel

The Lord make his face shine upon you and be gracious
to you.

—Numbers 6:25

I WAS TRAVELING IN my car on Georgia 400. Some call it the Speedway because people travel this highway, weaving in and out of traffic at a high rate of speed. It is the police officers' playground because they can so easily pluck a car from the road and issue tickets for speeding.

On this day like most, I had some place to go and a limited amount of time to get there. I was driving faster than I should have been going. Unfortunately, most of us go above the speed limit and just hope we slow down before it is too late. As I traveled down the highway, I could see flying through the air a giant piece of plastic. The sheet of plastic was the size of one you would remove from a new sofa. It was huge. It was drifting in the air, and now it was coming my way. I couldn't believe it!

Well, the giant wad of plastic landed softly on my windshield, forcing me to slow down so I could see and remain in my lane. I slowed down for a bit. After hitting my windshield, the plastic leaped over the top of my car. *How strange*, I thought. And then I saw something interesting—a police car with an officer pointing at drivers as they passed.

The wad of plastic, which caused me to slow down, actually prevented me from getting a speeding ticket. I had just encountered a plastic angel!

My Prayer and Praise: *Lord, thank You for slowing me down at the right time. Help me to drive safely with care and within the speed limit.*

Question to Ponder: Have you ever been snatched from the jaws of trouble of your making just in the nick of time?

Your Prayer: Ask the Lord to speak to your heart about living on the edge and the consequences of doing so. Write a prayer about it.

CHAPTER 10

Standing Up While Sitting Down

Do not let any unwholesome talk come out of your mouths, but only what is helpful for building others up according to their needs, that it may benefit those who listen.

—Ephesians 4:29

I WAS ON A full flight to Little Rock. Everything seemed to go as usual. Passengers were making their way down the aisle, placing their luggage in the overhead bins. Nothing unusual was going on. As the departure time grew near, the flight attendant began to make the usual announcements, asking us to buckle up, place items in the overhead bins, and move quickly so we could depart on time.

After the door closed, people continued to settle in. Then there was an announcement. There would be a slight delay because of a mechanical problem. The pilot explained the situation. And while it seemed like a fairly simple fix, according to him, he would have to go through their processes to handle the fix. After he promised to get back to us shortly, I could hear sighs and groans of discontent. I imagine people were concerned about layovers and other issues. And who likes to sit on the tarmac? People were obviously disappointed. However, they weren't as disappointed as the guy behind me. In fact, he hurled profanity for all of us to hear. A few minutes later, we got an update from the pilot. The guy behind me used more profanity. He started cursing and really didn't care who heard him. I looked around. Although people were annoyed, nobody wanted to take this guy on. They just didn't want to deal with this guy. However, it just didn't seem like he was going to let up with the profane talk.

I know it seems crazy, but I turned around and asked the guy to consider that we all can hear him. I went on to say, "Sir, we are all in this together." He did groan and grumble. And yet he did stop the profanity. In fact, he was as quiet as a church mouse from that point forward. While this guy was a brute, he made a decision to change the atmosphere. He realized he could do that by simply closing his mouth.

My Prayer and Praise: *Thank You for keeping me, especially when I feel like You are calling me to stand up. Lord, we sometimes don't realize how impactful we can be when we take a chance and stand up. When all others choose to sit, help me to take a stand.*

Questions to Ponder: Do you remain silent in fear of what will happen to you, even when you know you should say something or perhaps take a calculated risk? Are you a coward?

Your Prayer: Ask the Lord to give you the courage to stand up when it is time to stand up.

CHAPTER 11

God's Timing Is Perfect!

For you are great and do marvelous deeds; you alone
are God.

—Psalm 86:10

ISN'T IT AMAZING what can happen between the time you're standing in a line at the airport and what happens when you get to the counter? Traffic was bad that day, very bad, so it took longer than expected to get to the airport. I got in line. I knew I was cutting it close. On this day I didn't come prepared to carry on my luggage. I approached the counter to check my bag. The skycap said, "It's too late. You just missed the cutoff." That's English for "You're not going to make your flight." I remained calm. The skycap paused, looked at me, and said, "Come with me." I followed him through the sliding doors and up the stairs to the ticket counter. As I followed him, I began to pray, "Lord, please help me." A very nice colleague of his accepted my bag. I got a boarding pass and was on my way. I checked my bag and made my flight.

I wasn't supposed to make my flight, but I did. A simple prayer was answered. *Lord, please help me.* It's just another reminder that when things don't look good, when you get bad news, remain calm, pray, and let God handle it. And sometimes He will go beyond what we ask. I made my flight, and I got an upgrade.

My Prayer and Praise: *Lord, I thank You, and I praise You for all that You do. For me, it's a miracle. For You, Lord, it is just who You are.*

Question to Ponder: When an issue comes about—small, medium, or large—what do you do first?

Your Prayer: Ask the Lord to help you to bring Him to mind first when trouble comes. He might lead you to the right person. However, you have to seek Him first for the instructions.

CHAPTER 12

A Sea of Post-It Notes

And he said to them, "Go into all the world and preach
the gospel to all creation."

—Mark 16:15

IN RECENT YEARS, as the days have grown more evil, frankly, I began placing what I call large Post-it note prayers on the walls of my hotel room when I travel. These large notes contain life-affirming scriptures that remind me that God is with me. I had some tough moments here and there on the road as we all do, and so whether I was departing my room, entering, working, praying, or lounging, these scriptures reminded me that the Lord was and is on my side. In essence, walk by faith and not by sight. "We live by faith, not by sight" (2 Corinthians 5:7).

While staying at a hotel in Sea Island, Georgia, I placed scriptures on the walls as usual. This time, though, the encouragement was not just for me. Someone else needed it perhaps more than I did. Apparently, one of the associates at the hotel had been in my room to drop off a complementary dessert. I found out because during an inquiry I had of him about the hotel, he said, "I want you to know I was encouraged by the scriptures on the walls in your room." I told him I was glad to hear that. His comment led me to think about what people can perceive about us by simply walking into a hotel room where you're staying—the books and magazines on the nightstand, the food tray you left behind, what's on your bathroom counter, the medications you're taking, the clothes you wear, and the condition of the room. Is there anything about that hotel room we would not want others to know about? I don't know about you, but in the past I can honestly say that I didn't always read books or watch TV that edifies. In the past I did watch TV and read magazines that contained profane words, violent themes, and lustful situations. When I asked the Lord to cleanse my heart, He took all of these interests from my heart and out of my life. Thank You, Lord!

That room is more than a place to stay. It represents how we're living. Further, it also occurred to me after my phone conversation with the hotel employee that we are to live so that we can impact, encourage, and touch the lives of others. That can be anywhere—even in your hotel room. Most important of all, there is power in the name of Jesus and His Word.

My Prayer and Praise: *Lord, thank You for reminding me how powerful Your Word is—now and forever. Help me to use the power of the gospel of Jesus Christ to help reach a hurting world.*

Questions to Ponder: If guests stopped by for an impromptu visit, what would they see in your hotel room or your home? What kinds of books are you reading? What channel is your TV on? What kinds of movies are on your shelves? What's on your computer's search history? What kind of music are you listening to?

Your Prayer: Write here a prayer asking the Lord to lift anything out of your life that shouldn't be there. Ask Him to cleanse your heart, to perform heart surgery—if necessary, to remove any TV programs you shouldn't be watching, any books and magazines you shouldn't be reading, any words you shouldn't be saying, any relationships that need to be removed from your life. He'll do it if you're sincere and want to have a clean heart. He'll replace that space with sanctified actions that edify your life. Pray about it and be patient with yourself. Think about what it was like on moving day at your house. It might take some time to remove all of the junk from your life, but don't linger on it. Gather it all up and put out the trash and don't look back!

CHAPTER 13

The Bible

"Is not my word like fire?" declares the Lord, and like a
hammer that breaks a rock in pieces.

—Jeremiah 23:29

I WAS ON A flight from Miami to Atlanta. After the flight was on its way
and I was settled in, I started to read my Bible. It's not one of those
small, purse-size Bibles. It's a Daily Bible, and so it contains readings for
the whole year. In short, it's a big Bible.

The gentleman next to me asked, "What are you reading? The
dictionary?"

"No, the Bible," I said.

"I never see anyone read the Bible," he exclaimed. "Is it the whole
Bible?"

I said, "It is. It's a Daily Bible. I read it each day. When I'm finished
with it, I've read the entire Bible."

He shook his head and looked like he was taking in what I said. I
really wished I had said more. In fact, every now and then I think about
that brief dialogue, and I come up with all the things I could have said or
done. I could have opened the Bible, showed him some of the scriptures,
shared my favorite scriptures with him, and/or walked him through some
of the verses I underlined. I could have asked him about his relationship
with the Lord.

When you meet a stranger, especially on a flight, it is rare you will get
a second chance to share the gospel. Maybe that brief conversation was

enough. I'll never know, but God knows. The good news is that I am just a conduit, an instrument. The power is in God's hands.

My Prayer and Praise: *Lord, help me to remember that Your Holy Bible's power speaks for itself. Help me to shine its light. And when I have a chance to talk about Your word, help me to follow Your lead. I praise You for the precious gift of Your Word.*

Questions to Ponder: When was the last time you had a conversation with someone about the Bible? Have you ever taken it with you on a trip to read much like you do your other leisure books? If not, why? If someone filmed you for a week, how often would they see you read the Bible? If you have an interest in the Bible, a study Bible is a great place to start! For ideas, go to www.lifeway.com.

Your Prayer: Ask the Lord to help you pick up the Bible and read it daily. If you don't understand some of it, ask the Lord to give you understanding. The goal is daily study of God's Word. I once heard someone say, "A dusty Bible leads to a dirty life." I believe that. If you're not reading the Bible regularly, from where are you seeking godly counsel? What is your standard for guidance, direction, and wisdom?

CHAPTER 14

The Key

The Lord will keep you from all harm—he will watch over your life.

—Psalm 121:7

IT WAS COLD in Georgia, so it was good to be in Orlando, Florida, for a few days. Frankly, it was chilly for Orlando, and yet in spite of a little chill and a cool breeze, I decided to go for a run. On this day I wasn't wearing running pants with pockets, so I placed my room key in my sports bra. I've done it before, so I thought there was no harm. This room key was in a paper sleeve with my room number written on the outside. Good idea—unless you lose it. It is a slam dunk for the crooks.

Well, after running about a mile or so, I realized the key had fallen out of my sports bra. Why didn't I catch it on the way down? Why didn't I see it hit the ground? These are the questions I asked myself after I turned around and headed back to retrace my steps. I began to look around as I jogged back, but I didn't see the sleeve with the key in it. I looked carefully at the ground as I traveled at a slow pace. Where was it? Where could it be? Did someone pick it up? Will someone try to use it? Without a key, I'll have to go to the front desk and get another one … and ask them about the lost key. But wait! I don't have photo identification. How will I convince them that I am who I say I am? Just then at that moment, I saw on the ground a hotel key, but without the sleeve. *Thank You, Lord*, I said to myself. I believe this is my key. And the sleeve with my room number on it was somehow separated from the hotel key. I didn't see it anywhere.

Coincidence? I say no. There are no accidents in the kingdom of God. I skipped back to my room, and the key worked!

My Prayer and Praise: *Lord, even when I fall short, when I do goofy things—like take my safety for granted—You provide the best security system available, and that is Your divine protection. I praise You for keeping me safe in an unsafe world.*

Questions to Ponder: Can you think of a time when God provided safety and security for you and your family? Did you acknowledge God's hand on that situation?

Your Prayer: Write a prayer thanking the Lord for His divine protection— from that potential car accident, the time you tripped but didn't fall, the time you escaped the threat of danger.

CHAPTER 15

Divine Detour

All of us have become like one who is unclean, and all our
righteous acts are like filthy rags; we all shrivel up like a
leaf, and like the wind our sins sweep us away.

—Isaiah 64:6

IT'S ALWAYS INTRIGUING to see who you will sit next to when you're on
a flight. I was on my way to Little Rock, Arkansas. On this particular
flight, a pleasant man, probably in his thirties or forties, sat down next
to me.

After our flight departed, he struck up a conversation—just general
chatting and such. However, after a while, the conversation took a rather
interesting turn. Frankly, I am not sure how or why. After a few minutes, it
was becoming clear to me that this person was agnostic. It is my hope and
prayer that he has been transformed since our encounter. He seemed to be
rather cynical, frown on the things of God, and shun a godly perspective.
We talked about church, adoption, and a few other topics. I will protect
the details of our conversation. It is just safe to say though that he rejected
the ways of God and biblical principles.

After our conversation I looked out the window, grateful this
conversation was coming to an end. God had other plans. The flight had
to land at a small town's airport for refueling. This detour added at least
another thirty minutes or so to the journey. After refueling, the pilot had
to get the all-clear to depart, which took another fifteen to twenty minutes.

So I was on a flight that usually took no more than two hours but was now much longer, especially when I consider the resistance, the pushback and the defiance I was getting. After a few minutes of conversation along with the delay, I was ready to parachute from the plane to escape this conversation. But I was stuck. Frankly, I was struck by this man's unbelief. However, it is probably no different from who I used to be. I said I believed in God, but I wasn't saved. I didn't know Jesus as the Lord and Savior of my life. How was I any different from this guy?

Thank goodness I was sitting in a window seat so that I could just look out the window and ponder what to say or just not say anything at all. We continued to make small talk. The plane landed safely. As we hit the runway, I said, "Thank God." I know I was rubbing it in. I think he knew I was being sarcastic, and yet I often thank God for a safe trip, just not out loud.

When I arrived at my hotel, I walked into my room and immediately fell to my knees. I was so grateful to know God. I couldn't imagine living a life in doubt of who was in control. And I was so thankful for the gift of salvation. This divine detour was a reminder that people need to see the Jesus in us, even if it's hard for them to see Him at that time. The time I spent dialoguing also reminded me that so many people go about their lives, doing their own thing. They don't really think about God, and frankly, they don't want to hear about Him—unless there is a crisis. Still, we are called to stand up for the Lord. Instead of wanting out of the conversation, I now wish I had said even more to him about my faith. The Bible says, "But whoever disowns me before others, I will disown him before my father in heaven" (Matthew 10:33).

My Prayer and Praise: *I thank You, Lord, that I know You. Help me not to take my salvation for granted, especially in the midst of snide comments, cynicism, and persecution. I praise You that I once was lost but now I am found.* This conversation was a sobering reminder that I was once no different from the gentleman on the plane. *Lord, I once was a good person— no different from the agnostic—because I didn't know You personally, claim You as Lord and Savior, or enjoy a close personal relationship with You.* I was absent the gift of salvation. I was those filthy rags in Isaiah 64:6. Faith in Jesus Christ was my only hope. And it can be yours too.

Question to Ponder: Are you a good person? Have you accepted Christ as Lord and Savior of your life? If not, you can never be good enough. Christ is your only hope. Read John 3:16 out loud. If you are a believer, can you stand firm on the Word of God no matter who comes along with doubts, disrespect, or pure distain for God or the things of God?

Your Prayer: Ask the Lord to check your heart for a growing knowledge and understanding of Him. "The fear of the Lord is the beginning of wisdom, and knowledge of the Holy One is understanding" (Proverbs 9:10).

CHAPTER 16

New York, New York

And my God will meet all your needs according to the riches of his glory in Christ Jesus.

—Philippians 4:19

I T WAS TIME! I knew I would need a break soon, so when I was offered the opportunity to go to New York to see a Broadway play, I said yes! Before you know it, it was time to go. So I made all of the plans for me to meet up with a friend and the additional friends she invited. It was a group. I was looking forward to this quick pleasure trip.

I left for the airport. It was a rainy day, so traffic was heavy. It took longer to get to the airport than expected. Once there, I jumped out of the car and made my way to the foyer of the airport. It was there I realized I didn't have my driver's license. In this post-9/11 world, you absolutely can't do much without your driver's license. Rather than beat myself up for leaving my license at home, I decided I needed to use that energy to move forward.

Given the time it took for me to arrive at the airport, I knew there was not enough time for me to return home, come back, and catch my current flight. I knew I was going to have to change my current flight. How do I prove who I am without my driver's license?

I walked up to the ticket counter. I explained my situation to the representative. God immediately provided reinforcements. While I was standing there, a skycap I have known for years walked up to the counter. Keep in mind that I don't see him but every now and then. This skycap greeted me, embraced me, and said his usual friendly hello. He told me the representative at the counter would take good care of me. With his help, I made arrangements to get on the next flight. Wow! I had not seen this skycap in quite some time, but he showed up miraculously when I needed him to verify my identity just by walking up to the counter. He had absolutely no idea I was in a serious bind. I called my transportation and jumped in the car, and even with a relatively slow driver, I was able to make it back to the airport with a few minutes to spare. I made it to New York, Broadway, and back by Saturday morning.

My Prayer and Praise: *Lord, I praise You for meeting a need instantaneously. Even when I am forgetful, You come through for me. You don't sleep or slumber. Help me, Lord, to be reminded regularly of my need for You and Your grace. Amen.*

Questions to Ponder: What do you do when an emergency situation arises and you need quick action? How do you respond? Are you cool, calm, and collected? Or do you scream like the building is on fire?

Your Prayer: Ask the Lord to prepare your heart for emergencies—whether it's lost keys, a fender bender, or a health crisis. As you know, if you've not had an issue recently, it's only a matter of time before you'll be dealing with one. Prepare now. If you don't handle issues well, ask the Lord to give you calm when the storm comes.

CHAPTER 17

Woman on the Run

Submit yourselves, then, to God. Resist the devil, and he will flee from you.

—James 4:7

AT THE AIRPORT in Tampa, returning to Atlanta, I noticed a tearful young woman saying good-bye to a couple of people, perhaps family. We both made our way to security. She ended up behind me in line, and then later she was sitting next to me in the terminal as we waited for the same flight. She seemed a little nervous, and yet she was friendly. We began to talk. She shared that she was going to Atlanta to stay in a small town outside of the city to get away from the drugs and people who had helped to make her life difficult.

As she talked about her rugged, drug-induced, troubled life, she did say that she believed in Jesus. So I asked if we could pray right there in that busy terminal, and she said yes. So we grabbed hands right there in the gatehouse area with all of the noise, announcements, and people passing by. After we finished praying and chatting, we boarded the plane, each going to our own seats.

After the plane landed, I walked into the gatehouse area and waited for her. We walked toward the escalators, caught the train, and made our way to the terminal. I said good-bye and wished her well. She then met up with her family. They seemed glad to see her. I hope she received the desire of her heart to start over, drug-free.

My Prayer and Praise: *Lord, I praise You for the opportunity to join hands with those in desperate need of You. Thank You for this reminder that sometimes to start fresh, You have to make a run for it.*

Questions to Ponder: When a stranger confides in you, what do you do? In all likelihood, you will never see that person again, so how do you make that moment matter? Do you think it's an accident that you met him or her?

Your Prayer: Construct a prayer about seeking the Lord's divine wisdom quickly when you meet someone in desperate need of encouragement. You might be required to take action, offer encouragement, or simply say a prayer.

CHAPTER 18

Fat Wallet

Do not forget to show hospitality to strangers, for by
so doing some people have shown hospitality to angels
without knowing it.

—Hebrews 13:2

A FEW YEARS AGO, we went through a gasoline shortage in Georgia.
What I most remember is searching for stations with available gas.
These stations were easy to find. All you had to do was look for a crowded
station with horns blowing … and at times people arguing over who got
there first.

I decided to search for a place to get gas before going out of town. I
found a station on Old Milton Parkway. While there was a line, as I was
driving up, someone was pulling out. *Thank You, Lord,* I said to myself.
So I pulled out my credit card, got out of the car, and pumped gas. I
placed my credit card back in my wallet. I was so happy I found a station
without a lot of searching and seeking. I jumped in the car, pulled off, and
proceeded down Old Milton Parkway. I was down the street about two
blocks away from the station when I noticed someone behind me trying
to get my attention. What could she possibly want?

As I pulled up to the intersection in the left turn lane, the woman
behind me jumped out of her car while the light was red, came up to my
car, and proceeded to hand me my fat wallet, which had apparently been
on the trunk of my car and had been there for two blocks. I was about to
make a left turn, mind you.

Well, I was so excited about the gas that I wasn't paying attention, and I placed my wallet on the trunk and left it there. How does a fat, thick wallet stay on a slippery trunk for two blocks? The answer is that God saw fit for the wallet to stay on the trunk of my car for two blocks. Just imagine the woman behind me who saw this miraculous sight. She stepped in just in the nick of time. I was about to turn left. After she handed me my wallet, I thanked her over and over again. After we turned the corner, I could no longer see the car or the woman.

In the busyness of my day, God saw fit for an angel to be placed behind me at that perfect moment because the wallet would not have survived a left turn. And imagine what my day would have been like in anticipation of out-of-town travel—without my driver's license, credit cards, and other important items.

My Prayer and Praise: *Lord, I thank You and praise You for your perfect timing ... and for protecting my valuables.*

Questions to Ponder: Have you allowed God to use you to help someone out of a potential crisis he or she don't yet know about—a dropped wallet, a lost purse, potential danger the person is unaware of? Are you willing to help people in their time of unknown need, or are you satisfied that someone else will handle it? Have you ever been helped out of a bad situation before it occurred? If so, weren't you glad someone stepped in?

Your Prayer: Write a prayer asking the Lord to give you a spirit of helpfulness—if you don't have this attribute. You could be just that angel someone needs in their time of desperation.

CHAPTER 19

Football Fan

And the Lord's servant must not be quarrelsome; but must
be kind to everyone, able to teach, not resentful.

—2 Timothy 2:24

WHILE IN DALLAS on a business trip, I was staying at a Hilton
Hotel. It had been a long day. I was seeking peace and quiet.
While preparing for the next day, I started to hear noise coming from next
door. It didn't take long for the noise to get louder and louder. As I listened
more closely, it sounded like a man watching a football game—either alone
or with friends. It didn't matter. He was making enough noise for several
people. He was screaming, cursing, and perhaps even banging on a table.
It was just loud. I began to wonder if I was going to be able to live with
this noise late into the night.

The noise continued ... and continued. After a while, I decided I
wasn't going to be able to rest with all that noise. So as crazy as it sounds,
especially in this day and age, I decided to go knock on the man's hotel
room door. What was I thinking? Even now I am not sure what I was
thinking. Perhaps I should have just called the front desk and let them
handle it.

I left my room and proceeded next door. I knocked on the door. It
wasn't a hard, crazy knock on the door—just a normal couple of knocks.
And I didn't have a frown on my face because I knew the guy would look
through the peephole and see me. I stood there, smiling.

And then it happened. He opened the door. Guess what he said? "I'm too loud, aren't I?" I smiled. He said, "I am so sorry." We both smiled and chuckled a bit. I went back to my room, and he was as quiet as a mouse for the remainder of the night.

My Prayer and Praise: *Lord, thank You for keeping me in strange territory. We shouldn't always expect the worst. Thank You for kindness from a loud football fan. I praise You for the divine way in which You work and the armor of protection You provide to me when I need it most.*

Questions to Ponder: How do you respond to challenging, awkward situations that are almost impossible to ignore? This encounter was an opportunity to be pleasant rather than cranky, upbeat and positive rather than upset, and friendly instead of annoyed. God reached my heart and kept me. Has God ever delivered you from a potentially dangerous situation? Did your pleasant demeanor help turn away wrath?

Your Prayer: Ask the Lord to bring to mind any situations that could have ended negatively but didn't. Thank the Lord.

CHAPTER 20

A Novel Idea

For the word of God is alive and active, sharper than any double-edged sword.

—Hebrews 4:12

DON'T YOU JUST *love that middle seat?* It can be uncomfortable, a tight squeeze, and it is so hard to maneuver sitting between two people. It does serve a purpose though.

While sitting on the plane, I usually pass the time by reading or doing work. On this particular day, I chose to read my Daily Bible. On this flight I was in the middle seat, sitting next to a middle-aged woman with a pleasant face.

After the flight departed, she was leaning against the window, reading what looked like a romance novel. After a few minutes of reading and peaking over my arm, she asked if I was reading the Bible. I said, "Yes."

She said, "That's what I need to be reading. I don't need to be reading this junk." She was referring to her romance novel. "It's no accident I am sitting next to you," she said. From then on, we had a great conversation about the Bible and church. She committed to getting back to reading the Bible like she used to. She thanked me for our conversation and for the divine inspiration.

My Prayer and Praise: *Lord, thank You for your persistence. Sometimes You will move heaven and earth and speak through others to show us Your will.*

I praise You for the unique ways You reach us with Your Word. Help me to have a humble, open spirit so I can be used by You.

Questions to Ponder: Are you open to having conversations with strangers on a plane, or do you immediately send a signal that you can't be bothered? I am guilty of putting a wall up at times. I need to remember that God might have important work for me to do.

Your Prayer: Ask the Lord to give you the discernment to be open to dialoguing with strangers. It could change your life and the lives of others. Follow God's lead, and you could have a life-changing encounter!

CHAPTER 21

Divine Healing

But I will restore you to health and heal your wounds,
declares the LORD.

—Jeremiah 30:17

I TRAVELED TO MIAMI for a meeting. This was an important meeting that involved planning for a big annual event. When I arrived in Miami, I noticed that I had a slight itch in my upper torso area. What began as an itch turned into itchy, giant red patches that developed as a result of my scratching. I didn't want to panic. I just wasn't sure what I was reacting to that caused me such discomfort. I had visions of me going to the emergency room. Instead I started praying about the discomfort. I also walked to a nearby drugstore to purchase medication I thought would help me feel better.

The remedy was prayer and the medication. By the next morning, I was so much better. I later discovered that my skin reacted to a detergent with a harsh chemical in it. I was tempted to panic, and yet prayer on the road and a drugstore turned out to be the solution.

On another occasion I was out of town for a meeting. I had a freak accident involving a drinking glass. I picked up the empty goblet and attempted to move it, and it broke in my hand. Don't ask me how. The glass cut me on the palm of my hand. Let's just say it cut me just right and didn't cause severe injury. While there was blood, bandages, and a visit from hotel security out of sheer concern, the cut turned out to be minor. I did visit the doctor when I returned home, but it turned out that the aspirin

I had taken had caused it to bleed more than it would have normally. This situation could have ended badly, but it didn't. In fact, in both situations God was the divine healer.

My Prayer and Praise: *Lord, thank You for divine healing on the road. I praise You, God, for keeping me from panicking, from severe injury, and from disaster.*

Questions to Ponder: Have you ever experienced injury or sickness while traveling? What did you do? Did you pray before, during, or after your situation? Are there ways you would handle the situations differently in the future?

Your Prayer: Ask the Lord to prepare you for sickness or physical challenges during unexpected, unanticipated times and places. If it hasn't happened to you or your family yet, it's likely you will face a situation, accident, or illness in the future that will require divine healing.

CHAPTER 22

Called by Name

You are the God who performs miracles; you display your
power among the peoples.

—Psalm 77:14

TAKING A BUSINESS trip in late November can be hazardous to your
mental health. You're competing with Thanksgiving travelers, longer
lines, and just more activity. Was this a wise decision? Well, my goal was
to complete all of my agency reviews by the end of the year. I had three
left. My clever plan was to go from Tampa to Little Rock and then back
to Atlanta. I actually had to go back through Atlanta to get to Little Rock.
No worries—that's just travel! And I would check off my list two agency
reviews.

As I was landing in Tampa, I heard of a snowstorm heading to the
Southwest—Dallas, Oklahoma, and possibly parts of Arkansas. I had
traveled enough to know that when bad weather approaches, flights get
delayed all across the country. By the time my meeting ended in Tampa, I
had already changed my plans. I decided to go back to Atlanta and manage
my Little Rock meeting via conference call.

When I arrived in the security area, having just made changes to
my flight, I couldn't pull up my current boarding pass on my phone.
"Yikes," I said. I ran down to the ticketing area with my luggage in tow.
I approached a lady at the counter and tried to check in. "It's too late,"
she said. I explained to her that I couldn't retrieve my current boarding
pass on my phone perhaps because I had just changed my flight. She said,

"I'll see what I can do." She started typing quickly. She apologized for the trouble I had pulling up my boarding pass. She then handed me a boarding pass and said, "I can't guarantee you'll get on." I was concerned about the impending storm and flight delays left and right. I believed that if I didn't get on this flight, I might get stuck in Tampa overnight. Tampa was sunny and warm, even in November, but I didn't make plans to spend the night there.

I decided to make a run for it to the security area and jumped on the train. I got off the train and walked very quickly to the gate area. And then something happened that has never happened before. The kind representative at the counter had sent reinforcements. I heard a lady say my name out loud in the security area. She was looking for me. "Sheryl Sellaway," she said. I looked around, and I saw this short, pleasant woman with a booming voice actually calling my name. I identified myself to her, and she quickly helped me navigate through the security area. She stood with me as I checked in, hurried me through, waited on me as I went through the security line, and then walked very quickly with me to the gate. She even offered to carry my bag. She walked me up to the gatehouse and the check-in line. I thanked her over and over again. And as if that wasn't enough, I got an upgrade. I was so grateful and so thankful. I didn't know airlines did these kinds of things. Thank You, Lord, and thank you, Delta Air Lines!

My Prayer and Praise: *I thank You, Lord, for going above and beyond to help me reach my destination. You even sent help! I praise You for doing immeasurably more than I could ever ask or imagine (Ephesians 3:20).*

Questions to Ponder: When was the last time something happened to you that you could hardly believe? Did you credit it as luck? Did you thank the Lord or just the person who worked on your behalf because of the Lord?

Your Prayer: Write a prayer of thanksgiving for times when you got the last seat on the plane, the discount you received at a store that you didn't expect, or the unexpected kindness of a stranger on the phone. We often take these exchanges for granted.

CHAPTER 23

Twenty-Eight Hours

The righteous cry out, and the Lord hears them; he delivers them from their troubles. The righteous person may have many troubles, but the Lord delivers him from them all.

—Psalm 34:17, 19

I SURVIVED ATLANTA'S SNOW Jam of 2014—one of the worst snow and ice storms in Atlanta. This storm's icy roads caused the city to come to a screeching halt. Schools and offices closed, causing gridlock the city had never seen before. In fact, it took me ten hours to get home. I thought my travel navigating down eight miles of icy, slippery roads was quite a feat. Then I heard Sharon's story.

Sharon found out she had pneumonia on the day of the biggest, ugliest, most crippling storm in Atlanta to date. You see, Sharon had been fighting a cold/virus for approximately a month. She wasn't getting much better, and so she decided it was time to go to the doctor. The only appointment available was on that Tuesday, the day of the storm. The appointment was at 10:15 a.m. An hour later Sharon left her doctor's office and went to the hospital at 11:15 a.m. for chest X-rays at her doctor's request. At that time traffic was fine. The snow was just starting to fall. After Sharon left the hospital, she proceeded to the drugstore to pick up her prescription. At that time Sharon didn't realize people were starting to leave their offices. Parents were picking up kids, and stores were filling up with people preparing for the weather to come. And so a trip that should have taken thirty to forty-five minutes actually took eight hours. Sharon left the pharmacy at 9:00

p.m. She attempted to make it home, and within fifteen minutes she was in gridlocked traffic again. Sharon would go on to spend the next twelve hours in her car in temperatures between twelve to nineteen degrees. The next morning traffic moved just a little, and so she was able to make it to a gas station near the freeway. Sharon spent another six hours there until the freeway opened.

Sharon spent hours in cold weather that could have taken her life. She was unable to take the prescription medication because of the warning signs, including dizziness. Sharon is very thankful to God for how well He took care of her during those twenty-eight hours in her car. While Sharon was literally stuck with no place to go and nowhere to turn, she prayed, remained calm, and trusted God for His deliverance. His timing is always perfect.

My Prayer: *Thank You, Lord, for taking care of Sharon and many others with tremendous testimonies during Snow Jam of 2014. We praise You for keeping so many of us warm, safe, and free from harm.*

Questions to Ponder: Have you ever been literally stuck someplace with no way out? In a traffic jam, an elevator, or behind a locked door? What did you do, and who did you call on for help?

Your Prayer: Craft a prayer asking the Lord to help you manage your next crisis that will call for you to simply trust God. It's not a situation where you can hand over your credit card or make a phone call. You just have to pray and wait. Ask the Lord to give you divine wisdom, calm in the midst of the storm, and a way out.

CHAPTER 24

Duplicate Tickets

Take delight in the Lord and He will give you the desires
of your heart.

—Psalm 37:4

IMAGINE BEING IN an arena with thousands of screaming women. Well, that is what happens when you go to a popular women's conference. I went to see a few well-known speakers and to support a popular musical artist I happen to know.

I invited a friend from church, and we agreed to meet there. And we did. I met her at the door, and we went in. We had great seats on the floor—close to the front and in the center. After chatting for a few minutes, a couple of women arrived and had the exact same ticket numbers. This had never happened to me before, so it was a bizarre situation to be in. I texted the person who gave me the tickets, and she reached out to the floor manager for a solution. At the break we met up, and after a discussion I agreed to move to another area—to the right section of the floor seats. It was just a mix-up. It wasn't a bad spot—just not front and center. After we sat down and got comfortable, I realized I was sitting in front of a well-known author whose book I wanted signed for a business associate who was grieving the loss of a loved one. Perhaps, it was not a mix-up after all.

I said hello to the author and asked if he would sign the book. I told him who it was for. He said, "Sure, I'll sign the book." The problem was that I felt I should have purchased the book earlier but didn't. I ran to get the book, but when I returned, the author was gone. I decided to go to his booth. I sprinted to his booth. The associates working at his booth said he was already done signing books. Another lady said, "I am going to stand here just in case he signs more books." I decided I had nothing to lose. So sure enough, he did agree to sign more books.

When I reached the front of the line and asked him to sign the book for a particular person, an associate swooped in and said, "No, just a signature." I decided to remain calm. The author remembered me, asked me to step aside, and said he would sign my book specifically.

After a few minutes of waiting, the author did indeed sign the book personally for a person who was in great need of encouragement. The Lord placed me in the right seat at the right time to orchestrate the situation. It all began with the duplicate tickets. There are no accidents in the kingdom of God!

My Prayer and Praise: *Lord, when things don't seem to work as I planned, help me to pray and trust You to manage the details in ways only You can. I praise You, God, that You always do the amazing.*

Questions to Ponder: When there is a mix-up, do you see beyond it for a bigger purpose? How do you handle mix-ups? Do you get upset and make your response bigger than the issue at hand?

Your Prayer: Ask the Lord to place in your heart a desire to handle mix-ups with patience, kindness, and endurance.

CHAPTER 25

Wrong Room

He who conceals his sins does not prosper, but whoever confesses and renounces them finds mercy.

—Proverbs 28:13

I WAS IN NEW Orleans for a meeting. I checked in, looking forward to rest and relaxation for the evening. I proceeded to my room. I slid the key into the slot in the door. I walked into the room. After I was completely inside, I noticed that towels were on the floor outside of the bathroom. Someone was in the bathroom. Frankly, it scared me to death. I quickly backed out of the room, jumped on the elevator, and proceeded to the front desk. I told the individual at the front desk what happened. They were very apologetic. In fact, they gave me a beautiful suite for my inconvenience.

My Prayer and Praise: *Thank You, Lord, for sincere apologies for human error. I praise You for keeping me during the unexpected.*

Questions to Ponder: How do you handle human errors that inconvenience you? Do you treat people the way you want to be treated when they make mistakes? When people make mistakes, we choose how we treat them. Hopefully, we treat them the way we want to be treated in our own moments of failure.

Your Prayer: Ask the Lord to work on your patience and willingness to forgive quickly when people make mistakes, especially if you tend to be impatient.

CHAPTER 26

Stuck in the Middle

> Nor should there be obscenity, foolish talk or coarse joking, which are out of place, but rather thanksgiving.
> —Ephesians 5:4

I WAS SITTING IN that dreaded middle seat between two guys who obviously knew each other well. I was sitting between a conversation. I'd had a long day and was looking forward to returning home. It was time to relax. I decided to read the Bible. I pulled out my Bible and started reading. The conversation between the two guys continued with me in the middle. In spite of me reading the Bible, the guy in the aisle seat was talking to the guy in the window seat and using all kinds of profanity. I just couldn't believe I was trying to read the Bible while ducking and dodging, ignoring and fretting about the profane language. Couldn't this guy see I was reading the Bible? Where's the reverence for the Word of God? In his defense, I just don't think he was paying attention enough to realize I was reading the Bible. Plus whether I was reading the Bible or just sitting there, this guy's language was so much a part of him that he didn't consider that it might be offensive to others, and so he continued. He had no plans to alter his language. It never occurred to him to do so, and perhaps he hadn't yet been challenged to clean up his language.

After one of their dialogues, I very casually said, "Are you going to use profanity for the entire flight?"

The guy said in a nonconfrontational, innocent tone, "Was I using profanity?"

"Yes," I said.

"I didn't realize it. I will stop." And he did. He stopped immediately and seemed sorry about his words.

Sometimes people are so accustomed to doing or saying certain things that they don't even realize it, don't consider if it is offensive, and don't think about what it says about them. Old habits are hard to break.

My Prayer and Praise: *Lord, thank You for the opportunity to share the gospel in a unique way. I praise You for the opportunity to share my faith just by the way I respond to unflattering language.*

Questions to Ponder: How do you respond to offensive behavior? If you use profanity, even occasionally, have you thought about the impact it has on those around you? Do you care? Do you have any bad habits that the Lord would love for you to give up?

Your Prayer: Ask the Lord to help you find a way to address profane language in a nonconfrontational way. In this day and age, you'll definitely have the opportunity to practice what you pray for.

CHAPTER 27

Identity Crisis

Do not be anxious about anything, but in every situation, by prayer and petition, with thanksgiving, present your requests to God.

—Philippians 4:6

I WAS TRAVELING FROM Houston back to Atlanta. I was in a hurry. I had to deal with dropping off the rental car, catching the rental car bus, and checking my bag within the thirty-minute window. It was a hectic day! I dropped off the car and caught the rental car bus—no problem. However, when I got to the terminal near my airline's counter, I realized I had left my wallet on the seat in the rental car. My driver's license was in there. There was just no way I was going to check my bag in time to make the flight. So I stepped out on pure faith. I approached a woman at the counter and told her that I didn't have my license, which you absolutely need to check a bag at the airport. I explained to her what happened. She did what most wouldn't do. She checked my bag without a license. I then called the car rental company to attempt to get my wallet. The car rental's bus driver drove back to the airport with my wallet. I got it and ran to catch my flight. As I was running back by the airline's counter, I looked for the lady who was kind enough to help me but didn't see her. I made it to my flight.

My Prayer and Praise: *Thank You, Lord, for helping me out of a serious jam. I praise You for the kindness of strangers in critical moments when I desperately need help.*

Questions to Ponder: How do you handle serious jams, especially when time is of the essence? Do you expect others to drop everything and roll out the red carpet? Is your crisis everybody's crisis?

Your Prayer: Ask the Lord to help you to step out on faith quickly when needed.

CHAPTER 28

Shining a Light

No one lights a lamp and hides it in a clay jar or puts it
under a bed. Instead, they put it on a stand, so that those
who come in can see the light.

—Luke 8:16

I T'S A LONG flight from Atlanta to Orange County, California. It's
more than four hours. A lot can happen in four hours—a half day's
work, dinner and a movie, church and Sunday school, depending on the
church. Sitting in the middle seat on a long flight is no easy task. A lady
with an infant was on my row in the aisle seat. She wanted to sit next to
her friend in the row behind me, so she began trying to coordinate seating.
She asked me if I would mind moving from my window seat to the middle
seat behind me. Given the duration of this flight, I just couldn't move to a
middle seat on purpose. I remained in my window seat, and a young lady
came and sat next to me in the middle seat. We really didn't talk much at
first. I was reading and listening to music. She was sleeping.

About three hours into the flight, I talked to Ann, a young woman
sitting in the middle seat. She was smart and full of energy, especially
while talking about school and her area of study. She had plenty of plans
and seemed to know her path. Ann also spoke candidly about her life. She
alluded to some family problems and issues she's working through. You
see, she has a cleft lip along with two fingers on each hand instead of five.
She mentioned several surgeries and spoke of a particular surgery coming
up in a few months during the summer.

"God really has a purpose and plan for your life," I said.

Ann paused and said, "I am really not a religious person."

While her demeanor caught me off guard at first, I proceeded with the conversation. "It's not about religion. It's about knowing God, who has kept you through it all."

She said, "I did that. It was me."

She went on to say she felt uncomfortable, so I just said to her, "One day you will recall this conversation—whether it's a year or ten years from now."

I guess there are two ways to look at it. I have no idea how she feels when she examines herself. And I don't know how much she has endured. She might curse God or blame him for her challenges. I, on the other hand, in my naiveté thought she would give credit to God for keeping her all these years. I decided quickly that I had no idea how she felt, what she had been through, or what she saw up ahead for herself in the future. I just know that at that moment in spite of her confidence about school, she was desperately in need of faith. Her family troubles seem to weigh on her. She had more surgeries in her future, and she doubted the presence of God in her life. I did rest in the knowledge that God knew all about her situation.

After we walked off the plane and headed down to baggage claim, I hugged Ann and told her I would be praying for her. At that time, she probably wasn't sure exactly what that meant. When I think of Ann, I pray for her and hope I planted a seed that would be fertilized someday. You see, it was no accident that she was sitting next to me in that middle seat.

My Prayer and Praise: *Lord, help me to never take my relationship with You for granted. I praise You, Lord, that You didn't give up on me when I was in the wilderness. Some planted seeds. Some watered them, while others fertilized. And You, Lord, saved me. I pray this will happen to Ann and that one day she will rejoice to You that You indeed kept her all these years and that You affirmatively have a purpose and plan for her life. Amen.*

Questions to Ponder: What do you do when you encounter a person in need of faith?

Your Prayer: Thank the Lord for your faith. If you're lacking in faith, ask the Lord to reveal Himself to you, and He will.

CHAPTER 29

In Christ Alone

The Lord is a refuge for the oppressed, a stronghold in
times of trouble. Those who know your name trust in you,
for you, Lord, have never forsaken those who seek you.
—Psalm 9:9–10

WHILE IN ORLANDO, Florida, I jogged along a road with a
sidewalk, trees, and a few walkers here and there. I continued
to jog, observing children across the street waiting for a school bus, a row
of resort villas, and a few clouds in the sky.

After nearly an hour, I crossed a bridge and turned the corner, and
the sidewalk came to an abrupt end. Do I turn around, or do I continue
to run along a rather busy road in the grass, which is soaked because of a
steady rain the day before? I decided to continue.

The grass wasn't high, but the ground was soft and wet. The grass
contained hay, weeds, and cockleburs. It wasn't long before my pants
had cockleburs stuck to them. While the grassy road looked endless, I
continued to run, and before long, I reached a sidewalk again. It felt good
to hang in there and reach solid, predicable ground. At that moment I
realized that my life had been very similar. Everything was going along
smoothly, and then I hit unsteady ground.

While seeking the Lord, I also sought the help of others. Time and
time again with each encounter, God not only shut the door, but He
removed the knobs too. God was speaking to me very clearly. *Continue
to pray fervently, continue to seek Me out, trust Me and abide in Me, but do*

not seek out others for guidance, direction, or help unless I direct you to do so. Your help must come from Me. I am your only answer, your sole support, your only guiding hand, your only open door. Before long, I was on steady ground again. God indeed was my help, my shield, and my fortress.

My Prayer and Praise: *Lord, thank You for Your guiding hand during challenging times. Help me to stay close to You, seek You first, and look to You for divine guidance and direction.*

Questions to Ponder: What do you do when you hit a rough patch in your life? Perhaps you've been mistreated, or you're recovering from a bad relationship. Who do you talk to? How do you make wise decisions when you can't trust your emotions?

Your Prayer: Ask the Lord to build a firm foundation of faith in your life so that you're on solid footing when a crisis hits.

CHAPTER 30

The Letter

Dear friends, do not be surprised at the fiery ordeal that has come on you to test you, as though something strange were happening to you. But rejoice inasmuch as you participate in the suffering of Christ, so that you may be overjoyed when his glory is revealed.

—1 Peter 4:12

THIS IS ONE trip that didn't take me out of town. I traveled for miles and miles in my mind and in my heart to write a very difficult letter during a very challenging chapter in my life. I say chapter because in spite of the numerous challenges and circumstances, I always knew this season had a beginning, a middle, and an end. Like most of life's difficulties, I knew God would place a time limit on my pain. And like most valley experiences, I've always known that trouble doesn't last always.

So I sat down to write this letter. The first two versions of the letter were filled with facts as I saw them, explanations that contained elaborate details and some "he said, she said" complaints too. I knew the letter needed work, so I made revisions. I tore it up and made more changes to versions five and six. After some detailed edits, I asked the Holy Spirit if I should send the letter. My Spirit said, "No." After a couple of versions with yet more changes, I thought I was getting closer. However, when I prayed about it, I saw a clear picture that I believe was placed in my heart to show me the condition of the letter … and frankly, of my heart. It was a picture of a girl wearing a white sundress. She has a bat in her hand, and she's about to hit a beehive. Wow. That visual told me all I needed to know. The letter was stinging and could actually cause more harm than good. I either had to make significant changes to the letter before I could send it along, or perhaps the intent of the letter was to write the letter as a healing tool but not something to be sent. I continued to pray about the letter and its contents. Lord, do you want me to send the letter?

I worked on the letter again. This time I thanked those I sent the letter to for their help first. I acknowledged anything I could have done differently and outlined what I would do moving forward. This letter was radically different from the first one. I learned so much from this trip, and I actually sent the letter with God's blessing.

If you ask God for His help, He will help you from beginning to end. He will open your heart for self-examination, excavation, and deep cleansing. And He won't stop until you see yourself. After all, He allowed the situation that urged me to write the letter. He always has a purpose and a plan for all He allows in our lives. We just can't see it right then.

If we're seeking the Lord during the difficult times, studying His Word, and listening to His voice, He will guide, direct, and order our steps. He'll shed light on everything. You just have to be willing to look at what He sheds light on. The letter was just one tool God used to perform much-needed heart surgery. Even bigger than the letter, He revealed to me valuable lessons regarding the difficult situation. The trip was worth it!

My Prayer and Praise: *Lord, thank You for this journey. I've learned so much about myself. If I could place a sign on my heart, it would say, "Under Construction. We're making improvements so we can better serve You in the future." I praise You for the times in my life when you refined me so that I could be all that You've called me to be. Lord, You said we should "Consider it pure joy, my brothers and sisters, whenever you face trials of many kinds, because you know that the testing of your faith develops perseverance" (James 1:2). Help me to cling to the joy.*

Questions to Ponder: Have you ever had to write a difficult letter? Did you prayerfully consider what you should say, knowing that you couldn't take back your words once you mailed, hit send, or left behind a letter? What valuable lessons have you learned lately from a difficult situation?

Your Prayer: Letters, cards, and any heartfelt communication can be life-changing in a positive or negative way. Personal correspondence, especially the handwritten letter, is a lost art. Ask the Lord to bring to mind someone who desperately needs a letter of encouragement. Write to that specific individual the kind of letter you would like to receive in your time of need.

CHAPTER 31

Praising You Changes My Heart

Jesus replied: "Love the Lord your God with all your heart and with all your soul and with all your mind."

—Matthew 22: 37

And we know that in all things God works for the good of those who love him, who have been called according to His purpose.

—Romans 8:28

STANDING STILL. WAITING. Forgiving myself for bad decisions. Forgiving others for letting me down. Shedding the pride and arrogance from my life. Overcoming the missteps, the countless mistakes. A spotlight on my sins. Facing my shortcomings. Dealing with life's troubles, hardships, and difficulties. Fear. Pain. My past.

That's my pile of dirt. What is yours? These are just a sampling of rocks you can expect to unearth as you build a growing relationship with the Lord. Frankly, it's where God can do His best work. You see, He is not going to leave you the way He found you. The Lord has sharpened me through all of my brokenness, shame, and guilt, all of the ups and downs. If you will allow Him, He will do the same for you. In fact, He is going to use your difficulties to grow you, strengthen you, and equip you to be His servant and strong warrior for the Lord. He'll use the countless ways He has blessed you to encourage you, enlighten you, and increase your faith.

The Heart of the Matter

At the center of who we are is the heart. As I think about this very important organ of life and death, I can't help but think about how important the heart is to our physical, spiritual, and emotional existence. Let's examine a few scripture passages about the heart.

- ♥ "Trust in the Lord with all your *heart* and lean not on your own understanding" (Proverbs 3:5).
- ♥ "Above all else, guard your *heart*, for everything you do flows from it" (Proverbs 4:23).
- ♥ "I will give thanks to you, Lord, with all my *heart*; I will tell you of all your wonderful deeds" (Psalm 9:1).
- ♥ "May these words of my mouth and his meditation of my *heart* be pleasing in your sight, Lord, my Rock and my Redeemer" (Psalm 19:14).
- ♥ "The one who has clean hands and a pure *heart*, who does not trust in an idol or swear by a false god. They will receive blessing from the Lord and vindication from God his Savior" (Psalm 24:4–5).
- ♥ "Test me, LORD, and try me, examine my *heart* and my mind; for I have always been mindful of your unfailing love and have lived in reliance on your faithfulness" (Psalm 26:2–3).
- ♥ "The Lord is close to the broken*heart*ed and saves those who are crushed in spirit" (Psalm 34:18).
- ♥ "Take delight yourself in the Lord and he will give you the desires of your *heart*" (Psalm 37:4).
- ♥ "Create in me a pure *heart*, O God, and renew a steadfast spirit within me" (Psalm 51:10).
- ♥ "My flesh and my *heart* may fail, but God is the strength of my *heart* and my portion forever" (Psalm 73:26).
- ♥ "Blessed are the pure in *heart*, for they will see God" (Matthew 5:8).
- ♥ "For where your treasure is, there your *heart* will be also" (Matthew 6:21).
- ♥ "Jesus replied: Love the LORD your God with all your *heart* and with all your soul and with all your mind" (Matthew 22:37).

♥ "Peace I leave with you; my peace I give you. I do not give to you as the world gives. Do not let your *heart* be troubled and do not be afraid" (John 14:27).

♥ "And the peace of God, which transcends all understanding, will guard your *hearts* and your minds in Christ Jesus" (Philippians 4:7).

It has been said that happiness and a strong sense of emotional well-being helps lower our risk of heart disease. Wow. That means our heart has a lot more to say about who we are than we probably realize. Do you ever stop and think about the condition of your heart? That's a big question because in a day's time we experience so many emotions—ups, downs, joy, pain, frustrations, anger, hostility, happiness, sadness, and the list goes on. Do you care about the things God cares about, such as a personal relationship with Him, a pure heart, genuine love and concern, righteousness, integrity, honesty, truthfulness, sin, wickedness, bitterness, anger, ungodliness, and filthiness? Do you have a heart for the things of God? Why does God care about righteousness *and* wickedness, integrity *and* dishonesty? Well, because whatever takes up residence in your heart shows up in your life and either builds up or tears down the temple of the Holy Spirit. Righteousness produces right actions. Wickedness produces wrong, difficult, heart-wrenching actions. And when we sin, it impacts us individually and those around us.

As you ponder these questions about the condition of your heart, consider this. A heart that is hardened by sin cannot hear from God. That's because over time sin can cause the heart to be like stone, which means it becomes nearly impossible for the heart to feel anything that is of God. A person who engages in wickedness might feel some guilt at first, but if he continues with wicked actions, over time the voice of God seems farther and farther away. That's why it is so important to have a personal relationship with the Lord, study His Word daily, and repent of your sins. Think about it this way. Your heart is actually on display. While you might be able to disguise certain attributes about yourself, your heart eventually shows who you are—the good, the bad, and the ugly. Your heart engineers what you say, what you watch, what you listen to, what you allow in your life, the sacrifices you make for others, your motives, a desire to live a righteous life, and your loyalty to God and His Word. At times it can be a mixture of good and bad. Without a relationship with the Lord, the heart is in trouble—deep trouble. A sinful heart has endless room for so many emotions, behaviors, and thoughts that God abhors to take up permanent residence. If the heart is left unrepentant, the infiltration of wickedness can leave the heart numb. In fact, without the Lord's intervention, the heart can overflow with wickedness. That's why we desperately need Jesus. He is our only hope. The good news is that nothing is too hard for God.

As you consider matters of the heart, here are a few difficult yet reflective questions to ponder. They all relate directly to the condition of your heart.

1. Do you delight in the Lord or poke fun at those who do?
2. Do you use profane language often and ask others to forgive you as if it is okay?
3. Do you watch TV and movies that glorify wickedness, violence, profane language, and lustful actions but excuse it away as adult entertainment? What kind of music do you listen to?
4. How do you treat people who are unlike you? Do you give preferential treatment to those who are most like you? Do you profess to *love everybody* but show very little evidence of it in your outreach?
5. If you make a mistake that could impact you or someone else, do you tell the truth or let the other person take the fall?
6. Do you get angry with people for telling the truth? Do you believe it's okay to lie?
7. Do you pray with your family and friends? Is it evident you are a person of faith? When visitors come to your home, can they see evidence of your faith?
8. Do you seek revenge against others for doing what's right if it causes you trouble? Do you seek to repay evil for evil?
9. Do you step on others to advance your agenda or remain silent about something that is clearly wrong even if it causes others harm?
10. Do you read the Bible and yet make excuses for why you don't obey God's Word? Do you support efforts you know contradict God's Word?

11. Are you harboring ill feelings toward certain people because you think you're punishing them?

12. What do you treasure? God or the things of this world? Do you have time for hobbies but little time for the things of God? Examine your actions, not your words.

13. Do you take pride in ruling over others? Do you expect others to roll out the red carpet because of your status or position?

14. Do you give to those in need because it is God's desire that we help others, or do you give for the glory? Check your motives.

15. Do you pray and seek the Lord often, or do you wait until there is trouble on the horizon?

16. Do you apologize to people for your wrongdoings, or do you allow pride to reign on the throne of your heart and so refuse to do so?

17. When was the last time you talked about your faith outside your circle? Are you afraid to share your faith or give any indication you're a believer for fear of persecution?

18. Do you offer to pray for others when they're in trouble?

19. Do you give to your church and other organizations that preach the gospel of Jesus Christ?

20. Do you have the same standards for yourself as you do for others?

If you felt challenged by some of these questions, consider it an opportunity to ask God to cleanse your heart. Let's face it. We are all in need of open-heart surgery, so to speak. That's where God's unearned, unmerited grace, mercy, and forgiveness come in. That's where repentance comes in. Repentance is not just about being upset and sorry about your sin. It is expressing sorrow and allowing the Holy Spirit to reveal to you the depth of your sin and God's view of it. It's praying, seeking forgiveness, and expressing sorrow for what you've done. True repentance leads to a changed life. Only God can purify, cleanse, and perform supernatural, miraculous heart surgery so that we are changed and in such a way that it is evident to others.

Does your heart contain a few pebbles of wickedness that need to be sandblasted out of the crevices of your heart? Is your heart riddled with giant stones of unforgiveness and wrong actions? Or perhaps your heart has turned to granite from years of being far away from the things of God. If so, this is your opportunity to ask Him to transform you. A heart that is cleansed by God is a heart that can do unfathomable things for the Lord. A heart that is cleansed is a loving, kind, and giving heart. A clean heart changes relationships for the better. Your desire will change and bend toward the things of God. It will change what you want your eyes to see and ears to hear. A changed heart impacts all areas of your life. A heart for God impacts those around you ... and leads others to want to know Christ. A heart that loves God and His commandments is a cleansed heart. Don't let your heart get in the way of you loving God and others. God can't use a wicked heart.

First, determine in your heart if you know Jesus as Lord and Savior. If you have given your life to Christ and have simply fallen away from the faith, ask the Lord to cleanse your heart right now. Invite the Holy Spirit to speak to your heart. "But the Advocate the Holy Spirit whom the Father will send in my name, will teach you all things and remind you of everything I have said to you" (John 14:26). The Holy Spirit will use the Word of God to supernaturally reveal to you the areas that need work. Even if your thoughts or beliefs contradict with the Word of God, don't give up. God wants to mold you spiritually so that you will draw closer to Him and align with His Word. If you want God's best for your life, see it as a journey. Trust the Lord to change, strengthen, and grow you with the truth of His holy Word. Consider this warning: Praying this prayer that follows will change your life in ways you never imagined. Expect miracles.

> Thank You, Lord, for calling on me to examine my heart. I want a heart that honors You. I want to put You first, to be loyal to You.
>
> Please forgive me for times when I allowed sin, unforgiveness, wickedness, anger, frustration, bitterness, and callousness to rule and reign in my heart.
>
> Lord, I have hurt You, others, and myself. Please perform heart surgery right now. Break up the fallow ground, remove the weeds, the rocks, the stones, the hurt, the pain. Replace the unearthed dirt with a clean heart and a desire to obey you, repent of my sins, study Your Word, care about others, forgive, and be forgiven.

Help me to love You with all my heart, all my soul, and all my mind. Please cleanse my heart of any unrighteousness and hold me accountable for repenting of my sins so that continuous, life-changing cleansing takes place. Further, please lay on my heart any matters that need to be addressed so that I can place those petitions on the altar and proceed to have right fellowship with You. Lord, with an eagerness to serve You, I look forward to all the magnificent ways You will work in my life with a clean heart. I ask all these things in Jesus's holy name. Amen.

Challenge yourself. In a few months, return to this section, revisit the questions, and reflect on your responses. If there's a heart change, great. Thank God and continue this difficult work. Stay in prayer about the issues that continue to challenge your heart, especially as they relate to truthfulness, honesty, integrity, and righteousness. Your heart is in trouble without these important vessels. This is a very difficult, emotional undertaking. Your sinful nature will battle with your work to put God first. That's why it's so important to devote time and energy to praying and studying God's Word while seeking out specific scriptures that help you respond to matters of the heart.

In addition to praying and studying God's Word, it is just as important to listen to God. It's a divine opportunity to hear from Him. He might reveal unconfessed sin, a scripture to apply to your life or important next steps on your journey. If you do all of the talking, you might miss the important wisdom and direction God has for you. In the quietness of just sitting before the Lord without any distractions, allow Him to speak to your heart in a way only He can. "Blessed are those who listen to me, watching daily at my doors, waiting at my doorway. For those who find me find life and receive favor from the Lord. But those who fail to find me harm themselves" (Proverbs 8:34–36).

Address any issues that God places on your heart. He might require you to seek out those you have hurt to ask for forgiveness. This is tough. Lay aside your pride. This is potentially a step in the cleansing process. Praise God for His divine intervention, grace, mercy, and unconditional love for you. Don't be afraid to pour your heart out to the Lord. He already knows your story. Just remember that real change is evident to others. It's a lifetime journey! "But seek first his kingdom and his righteousness, and all these things will be given to you as well" (Matthew 6:33).

Are You a Member of the Kingdom of God?

My encounters with people on the road during my travels were divine moments. You've had them too. The rich, priceless experiences I had were designed to teach me valuable lessons, help me to see matters from a different, more empathetic point of view, and help others to see God in a hurting world. Jesus paid an awful price, but at the same time it was an awesome price He paid for our sins so that we could become righteous. He is the divine teacher, Counselor, and Comforter—the God of the universe. It is incredibly difficult to deal with the dirt in our lives, and yet the blessing is that God can wash it away and use it for your good and His glory in His perfect timing.

Standing still. Waiting. Prayer time. Sins forgiven. Thanksgiving for life. Joy. Peace. Willingness to forgive those who hurt you deeply. Divine protection. Contentment. Generosity. Helping others. A desire to wait on the Lord. Daily study of God's Word. Using words that edify. Encouragement. Enjoying God's magnificent creation. Honesty. Integrity. Truthfulness. A desire to walk with the Lord, not the world. Caring about others. Love for all of God's children. God's love casting out fear. No longer a slave to sin. Protection from your enemies. Blessed by brokenness. A willingness to stand up for the Lord even if it means losing jobs, putting relationships in jeopardy, and being an outcast. A willingness to be persecuted. Praise. Worship. An imperfect child of the Most High.

These are just a few of the innumerable benefits of being a member of the kingdom of God. Membership definitely has its privileges. Some might say a few of these benefits don't feel much like benefits, namely persecution. What I've come to know is that it's all good. It's all for a reason and a season. The Bible says, "But rejoice that you participate in the suffering of Christ, so that you may be overjoyed when his glory is revealed" (1 Peter 4:13). We are to rejoice. And the Bible also says, "You intended to harm me, but God intended it for good to accomplish what is now being done, the saving of many lives" (Genesis 50:20).

If you're a mature believer in the faith, it's likely you have a few battle scars from the journey. It's not an easy walk. In fact, it's very challenging to align with the Word of God in a secular world. It's not enough to enjoy the privileges of being a Christ follower. We are called to follow *and* to lead others to Christ. As you travel along this lifelong journey, be sure to link arms with other believers and those new in the faith to offer support, words of encouragement, and the truth according to the Word of God.

Remember, through all of your ups and downs and trials of various kinds, God didn't send His Son to condemn us. He sent His Son to save us—all of us. Like it or not, God allows the good, the bad, the ugly, the sunshine and the rain for our good and His glory. Praising You, Lord, changes me and my heart. And it can change you too! "Now to Him who is able to do immeasurably more than all we ask or imagine, according to his power that is at work within us" (Ephesians 3:20).

To him who is able to keep you from stumbling and to present you before his glorious presence without fault and with great joy—to the only God our Savior be glory, majesty, power and authority, through Jesus Christ our Lord, before all ages, now and forevermore! Amen.

—Jude 24–25

CHAPTER 32

Praising You Changes Me: Twenty Proclamations I have Learned about God

T HE MORE I mature in my faith, the more I have come to know about the character of the Lord. These twenty proclamations are reflective of those learnings. I gained these insights by studying God's Word daily, praying, listening to the Lord, participating in Bible studies, weekly church services, worship and praise opportunities, and waiting upon the Lord for direction and guidance in all areas of my life.

1. *We serve a God who wants us to have a personal, saving relationship with Him.* God doesn't want our rituals, signs of religion. He wants our relationship with Him to be obvious by the way we live out our faith. His presence in our lives should be evident for others to see. "If you love me, keep my commands" (John 14:15).

2. *We serve a holy God who wants first place in our heart and our lives.* Only God is perfect. And yet as Christ followers, He does expect us to live holy lives. If our actions conflict with the Word of God, we may actually turn others away from Him instead of draw them close to Him. Holy means set apart. God wants us to be set apart. "But just as he who called you is holy, so be holy in all you do; for it is written: 'Be holy, because I am holy'" (1 Peter 1:15).

3. *We serve an unchanging God.* God expects us to change, mature, and grow as our relationship with Him changes, matures, and grows. And yet He never changes. God and His Word are irrefutable, undeniable, and inerrant. "Jesus is the same yesterday, today and forever" (Hebrews 13:8).

4. *We serve a God who wants us to forgive our enemies and those who persecute us.* The world loves revenge. God demands that we love our enemies and let Him carry out actions against those who mistreat us as He chooses, how He chooses, and in His timing. "For if you forgive other people when they sin against you, your heavenly father will also forgive you. But if you do not forgive others their sins, your Father will not forgive your sins" (Matthew 6:14–15).

5. *We serve a God who created the heavens and the earth.* God wants us to enjoy the majestic beauty of His creation. When we rejoice in the glorious sun, the deep blue sky and seas, the moon and countless stars, the highest, most amazing mountains and astonishing views that take our breath away, we are to worship God, giving all gratitude, honor, and praise to Him and not creation, for they are all His. "For by him all things were created: things in heaven and on earth, visible and invisible, whether thrones or powers or rulers or authorities; all things were created by him and for him. He is before all things, and in him all things hold together" (Colossians 1:16–17).

6. *We serve a jealous God.* God is not interested in an informal, casual relationship with us because He knows a heart that is uncommitted to Him is troubled, distant, and wicked. God doesn't want to be second place, plan B, or an outcry only when there is trouble. He wants us to reverence Him. "For the Lord your God is a consuming fire, a jealous God" (Deuteronomy 4:24).

7. *We serve a God who is loving, merciful, and gracious and rewards righteousness.* Righteousness—it's not a word you hear much in our society. And yet righteousness is very important to God. In fact, several versions of this word are mentioned in the Bible more than five hundred times! "Even in the darkness light dawns for the upright, for those who are gracious and compassionate and

righteous. Good will come to those who are generous and lend freely, who conducts their affairs with justice. Surely the righteous will never be shaken; they will be remembered forever. They will have no fear of bad news; their hearts are steadfast, trusting in the Lord. Their hearts are secure, they will have no fear; in the end they will look in triumph on their foes" (Psalm 112:4–8).

8. *We serve the Sovereign God of the universe.* He holds it all and owns it all. He is omnipotent, omniscient, and omnipresent. He is the Alpha and the Omega. The beginning and the end. "Remember the former things, those of long ago; I am God, and there is no other; I am God, and there is none like me. I make known the end from the beginning, from ancient times, what is still to come. I say: My purpose will stand, and I will do all that I please" (Isaiah 46:9–10).

9. *We serve a God who loves the sinner and hates sin.* God wants us to confess our sins and repent so that He can forgive us and cleanse us of all unrighteousness. "If we claim to be without sin, we deceive ourselves and the truth is not in us. If we confess our sins, he is faithful and just and will forgive us our sins and purify us from all unrighteousness" (1 John 1:8–9).

10. *We serve a God who blesses us so we can bless others.* Here's a news flash: Everything good comes from God. He makes it clear in His Word that He wants us to bless others just as He blesses us. You could be the answer to a prayer! "In the same way, let your light shine before others, that they may see your good deeds and praise your Father in heaven" (Matthew 5:16).

11. *We serve a God who wants us to wait upon Him.* Do you want God's best? If so, it is far better to wait upon Him—His will for your life—because He knows best. While you might get your way through lies and deceitful actions, manipulations, hurting others, stealing, or using your power or position to get your way, anything you acquire outside of God's will ultimately turns to ashes. "Since ancient times no one has heard, no ear has perceived, no eye has seen any God beside you, who acts on behalf of those who wait for him" (Isaiah 64:4).

12. *We serve a God who will not be mocked.* When man disrespects, disregards, and dishonors God, there are consequences. "Do not be deceived: God cannot be mocked. A man reaps what he sows" (Galatians 6:7).

13. *We serve an all-powerful, all-knowing God.* He sees it all and knows it all. You can't hide from the Lord. "The eyes of the Lord are everywhere, keeping watch on the wicked and the good" (Proverbs 15:3).

14. *We serve a God who wants us to share the gospel.* There are three ways to share the gospel—by our walk, our ways, and our words. "All Scripture is God-breathed and is useful for teaching, rebuking, correcting, and training in righteousness, so that the servant of God many be thoroughly equipped for every good work" (2 Timothy 3:16–17).

15. *We serve a God who believes you can't fully know Him if you don't believe and don't study His Word—the Holy Bible.* I once heard someone say, "A dusty Bible leads to a dirty life." How can you obey the Lord if you refuse to study His Word? "Keep this Book of the Law always on your lips; meditate on it day and night, so that you may be careful to do everything written in it. Then you will be prosperous and successful" (Joshua 1:8).

16. *We serve a God who wants us to love Him with all our heart, all our soul, and all our mind.* God wants first place in our lives. He is not satisfied with any other position. He wants to be the chairman and CEO—our first, last, and everything! While the world idolizes man and his humanity, God believes you can't serve two masters. You will love one and hate the other. "Jesus replied: 'Love the Lord your God with all your heart and with all your soul and with all your mind.' This is the first and greatest commandment" (Matthew 22:38).

17. *We serve a God who allows rain to fall on the righteous and the unrighteous.* Our God is an equal opportunity God. He loves us all. Righteous or unrighteous, we will all face challenges. It is more comforting to bear our burdens with the Lord's help. "He causes his sun to rise on the evil and the good, and sends rain on the righteous and the unrighteous" (Matthew 5:45).

18. *We serve a God who sits high and looks low.* At times it is easy to forget that we have a God who sees it all—everything. "Though the Lord is exalted, he looks kindly on the lowly; though lofty, he sees them from afar" (Psalm 138:6).

19. *We serve a God who never gives up on us.* God is always there. He doesn't leave us, and we leave Him. He is faithful. "Have I not commanded you? Be strong and courageous. Do not be afraid; do not be discouraged, for the Lord your God will be with you wherever you go" (Joshua 1:9).

20. *We must serve Jesus as Lord—God the Father, the Son, and the Holy Spirit.* It's one thing to believe in God. It makes all the difference in the world from now until eternity—to believe in God and to accept Jesus Christ as Lord and Savior and the gift of the Holy Spirit. We serve a triune God. "But when the kindness and love of God our Savior appeared, he saved us, not because of righteous things we had done, but because of his mercy. He saved us through the washing of rebirth and renewal by the Holy Spirit, whom he poured out on us generously through Jesus Christ our Savior, so that, having been justified by his grace, we might become heirs having the hope of eternal life" (Titus 3:4–7).

CHAPTER 33

Can You Accept a Free Gift?

HAVE YOU HEARD the good news of the gospel of Jesus Christ? The good news is you can receive the free gift of heaven. You can't earn this gift. You can't receive this precious gift through good works. Heaven—this gift of eternal life—can only be received through faith in Jesus Christ. Specifically, it is a saving faith that trusts in Jesus Christ alone.

God loves us all, and yet He knows that we have all sinned and fallen short. The only person who lived without sinning is Jesus Christ. The Bible says the wages of sin is death. Because we can't die for our own sins or do anything to make ourselves right with God, Jesus became a human being to die in our place. He died on the cross and then was resurrected, proving that His death on the cross was enough. Jesus took the burdens of all our sins on Himself and died in our place in payment for our sins. He overcame sin and death for us all.

So if you want to know what you must do to be saved and receive the gift of salvation through faith in Christ, it is simple. Give your life to Jesus Christ. Here are five scriptures that will help you grasp more insight about this precious gift of heaven through faith in Jesus Christ.

1. *There's the gift of eternal life.* "For the wages of sin is death, but the gift of God is eternal life in Christ Jesus our Lord" (Romans 6:23).
2. *There's only one way to salvation.* "Salvation is found in no one else, for there is no other name under heaven by which we must be saved" (Acts 4:12).

3. *We are all sinners.* "For all have sinned and fall short of the glory of God" (Romans 3:23).

4. *Believe in Jesus Christ and receive salvation.* "Sirs, what must I do to be saved? They replied, 'Believe in the Lord Jesus, and you will be saved'" (Acts 16:30b, 31).

5. *Jesus died for our sins because of His love for us.* "For God so loved the world that he gave his one and only Son, that whoever believes in him shall not perish but have eternal life" (John 3:16).

The Bible says in Acts 2:21, "And everyone who calls on the name of the Lord will be saved." You can give your life to Christ today by talking to the Lord right now. While you can't receive salvation by simply reciting a prayer, you can accept and believe in Christ and trust Him as your Lord and Savior by placing faith in Jesus Christ and accepting Him into your heart. If you believe in Jesus Christ and accept Him as your Lord and Savior, here is conversational prayer to the Lord.

A Conversational Prayer with the Lord about Your Salvation

I acknowledge today that Jesus Christ is God, the Father, the Son, and the Holy Spirit. He lived as man on this earth and lived a sinless life. He died on the cross and shed blood for my sins so that I wouldn't have to pay for them. He rose from the grave to purchase a place in heaven for me.

I confess to You, Lord, that I am a sinner. Please forgive me for my sins and cleanse me of any unrighteousness. Please forgive me for times when I have lived for myself and have been disobedient toward You.

I am now ready to trust You, Jesus, as Lord and Savior. I'm asking You, Jesus, to please come into my heart and be the Lord of my life so that You can live in my heart now and for all eternity. Please save me.

I place my trust in You, Lord, for my salvation, and I joyfully accept this gift of eternal life. In Jesus's holy name. Amen.

Romans 10:9–10 says, "If you declare with your mouth, 'Jesus is Lord,' and believe in your heart that God raised him from the dead, you will be saved. For it is with your heart that you believe and are justified, and it is with your mouth that you profess your faith and are saved." If you accept these words into your heart, your life will never be the same. Find a Bible-believing church, study God's Word, and watch the Lord work in your life—now and forever!

Who, being in very nature of God, did not consider equality with God something to be used to his own advantage; rather, he made himself nothing by taking the very nature of a servant, being made in human likeness. And, being found in appearance as man, he humbled himself and became obedient to death—even death on a cross! Therefore God exalted him to the highest place and gave him the name that is above every name, that at the name of Jesus every knee should bow, in heaven and on earth and under earth, and every tongue confess that Jesus Christ is Lord, to the glory of God the Father.

—Philippians 2:6–11

CHAPTER 34

The Journey Never Ends: Praising You Changes Me Forever

I am the true vine, and my Father is the gardener. He cuts off every branch in me that bears no fruit, while every branch that does bear fruit he prunes so that it will be even more fruitful. If you remain in me and I in you, you will bear much fruit; apart from me you can do nothing.
—John 15:1–2, 5

I AM SO THANKFUL to the Lord for all the divine moments I had on the road. The countless strangers I met, the endless and boundless blessings I received over and over again, and the numerous challenges I encountered all worked in my favor. You see, these true stories allowed me to see God's hand over and over and over again. We should never take for granted the chance meetings we have because chances are that they are not chance meetings after all. Rather, they are God's opportunities to bless us, grow our faith, build us up, wake us up, prune us, and strengthen our faith. "And we know that in all things God works for the good of those who love him, who have been called according to his purpose" (Romans 8:28).

A Closing Prayer

Most gracious, holy, and loving God, I thank You for the divine opportunity to meet you on the road in so many places. Praising You changes me.

I thank You for being the Sovereign God of the universe. There is none like you, Lord. You own it all and hold it all. Every good thing comes from You. You are the beginning and the end, the Alpha and the Omega, first, last, and everything. You're my Rock, my Deliverer, my Redeemer, King of Kings, and Lord of Lords. You are the way, the truth, and the light. You never change.

Thank You for keeping me during the difficult times, the moments of persecution that don't compare to Your walk on this earth or Your death on the cross.

Thank you for not leaving me where You found me—lost. Rather, I praise You, Lord for transforming my heart so that I can hear from You, embrace the power of your holy Word, and forgive—so that I can be forgiven.

Lord, when I am tempted to place my hope in the things of this world, please remind me that I am Yours first.

During joyous days, help me to exclaim of Your magnificence. During the storms of life, help me to cling to You with all my might, no matter my circumstances. Help me to say, "I trust You, Jesus." Thank You, heavenly Father, for helping me to fight my battles on my knees. Help me to walk by faith and not by sight.

I know in this world I will have trouble. You said so. Help me to remember that trouble doesn't last, for You always have a purpose and plan for all You allow in our lives. I know You won't place more on my shoulders than I can bear. I know You have placed a time limit on my pain.

This earth is not my home, Lord, so help me not to hold on too tight but rather to live for You, study Your holy Word daily for divine direction, and seek out Your will for my life.

I thank You and praise You for being the great I Am. Help me to never forget that the joy of the Lord is my strength and my shield (Psalm 28:7). I pray all these things in Jesus's holy name. Amen.

Tools for Your Journey

Travel Mercies: Praising You Changes Me on the Road

God's Word covers all areas of our lives, including travel on the road. Whether by car, airplane, or train, near or far, we all need travel mercies. Here are a few comforting scripture passages for times on the road.

Deuteronomy 28:6 says, "You will be blessed when you come in and blessed when you go out."

Isaiah 58:11 says, "The Lord will guide you always; he will satisfy your needs in a sun-scorched land and will strengthen your frame. You will be like a well-watered garden, like a spring whose waters never fail."

Psalm 4:8 says, "In peace I will lie down and sleep, for you alone, Lord, make me dwell in safety."

Psalm 5:12 says, "Surely, Lord, you bless the righteous; you surround them with your favor as with a shield."

Psalm 32:8 says, "I will instruct you and teach you in the way you should go; I will counsel you with my loving eye on."

Psalm 37:23 says, "The Lord makes firm the steps of the one who delights in him; though he may stumble, he will not fall, for the Lord upholds him with his hand."

Psalm 91:10–11 says, "No harm will overtake you, no disaster will come near your tent. For he will command his angels concerning you to guard you in all your ways."

Psalm 119:133 says, "Direct your footsteps according to your word; let no sin rule over me."

Proverbs 3:6 says, "In all your ways submit to him, and he will make your paths straight."

Matthew 21:21–22 says, "Jesus replied, 'Truly I tell you, if you have faith and do not doubt, not only can you do what was done to the fig tree, but also you can say to this mountain, "Go, throw yourself into the sea," and it will be done. If you believe, you will receive whatever you ask for in prayer.'"

Ephesians 3:20 says, "Now to him who is able to do immeasurably more than all we ask or imagine, according to his power that is at work within us."

James 1:5 says, "If any of you lacks wisdom, you should ask God, who gives generously to all without finding fault, and it will be given to you."